MY KITCHEN

CASUAL HOME COOKING
PETE EVANS

MY KITCHEN

CASUAL HOME COOKING

PETE EVANS

MURDOCH BOOKS

CONTENTS

INTRODUCTION

Over the last five years I have spent less time in my commercial kitchens during the night-time dinner service and a lot more time at home cooking for my family and friends. This has come about for a few reasons, the first being that I have simplified my approach to cooking in my businesses: I no longer try to keep up with the Joneses, so to speak, always trying to reinvent the wheel with the dishes I create. I did that for 10 years and achieved what I wanted in that time, so these days I instead focus on utilising amazing produce, treating it with respect and cooking it simply to let the true nature of the ingredients speak for itself. I also think that people today want more honest food when they eat out, with fewer hands involved in getting the meal to the plate; one result of this approach is that eating out becomes a lot more affordable.

However, that said, the number one reason for spending a lot more time at home in my kitchen is definitely to enjoy as much time as possible watching my kids grow up. I love to be at home to cook them their dinner and watch their young palates evolve and develop. I have only one rule for my kids when eating, and that is that they need to try at least one bite of something; if they don't like it, then they don't have to eat it again that night, but they will have to try it again a month or so later. The kids are happy with my approach. I get so excited when one of my children tries something they haven't liked before and instead of the usual response, 'Yucky, Dad' they do a U-turn and say, 'Yummy, Dad'. It really brings a smile to my face when this happens, not only because it means that the more foods they like the easier it is for me in the kitchen, but also because I want them to experience the joy of food in all its beauty: the taste (spicy, salty, sweet, sour), texture (crunchy, slippery, chewy, unctuous), aroma (fragrant, tantalising) and the visual beauty of a dish.

Another reason why I love cooking in my kitchen at home is that I can experiment with different cuisines in a way that I can't necessarily do in my restaurants. The greatest thrill of being a home cook rather than a chef is that I can be as creative as I like and have no restraints. That is why it has been such a pleasure writing this book, as I have been able to include some of my favourite and most enticing recipes created in my kitchen over the past 20 years, as well as including some of the recipes my mum used to feed me before my culinary career started. I think it is so important to pass on knowledge (in this case recipes) to the next generations and cooking is a great way to teach your kids or grandkids the importance of food in our everyday lives, not only as a way to fill our bellies, but also as a way to get the family unit together and celebrate each other's company.

This book has been broken into some basic chapters: breakfast, vegetarian, seafood, poultry and meat, lunches and dinners, side dishes and, of course, desserts. The recipes are what I consider to be excellent week-night choices for the busy home cook and as always with my books I have about 20 percent of them designed for the more serious cook who has a bit more time on their hands. Some of the recipes you will need to think about in advance and let marinate overnight while others don't take much preparation but need a long time to cook in the oven. You can rest assured that these recipes have been tested by the fiercest critics known to me—my friends and family and, as with all the books I have written, if it doesn't taste yummy to them then it doesn't end up in the book. If you take just one recipe from this book and incorporate it into your cooking repertoire then I know all this hard work has been well worth it! I love to hear your stories about either your experiences with my recipes or, more importantly, yours. If you feel like letting me know, shoot me an email at info@peterevanschef.com.

Cheers, Pete

BREAKFAST

01

BIRCHER MUESLI WITH LSA MIX

4 SERVES

200 g (7 oz/2 cups) rolled (porridge) oats
1 tablespoon LSA mix (see Note)
250 ml (9 fl oz/1 cup) milk
250 ml (9 fl oz/1 cup) apple juice
juice of 1 lemon
1 tablespoon ground apricot kernels
   (optional)
2 apples, coarsely grated
1 banana, chopped
125 g (4½ oz/1 cup) mixed berries
   (blackberries, blueberries, strawberries
   and raspberries)
3 tablespoons chopped walnuts
4 dried apricots or dried figs
3 tablespoons organic honey
1 tablespoon sesame seeds
1 tablespoon pepitas (pumpkin seeds)
125 g (4½ oz/½ cup) plain yoghurt
8 mint leaves
fresh honeycomb, for garnish

A little while ago, I was fortunate enough to do some work for one of the leading spa resorts in the world and, as payment for my services, I spent a week in Thailand at their Six Senses Sanctuary Spa in Phuket. Wow, what a place! For a week I did nothing but yoga, pilates and gym sessions, went scuba diving with manta rays and sharks, and ate the most delicious organic food. In fact, it was some of the best food I have ever had, not to mention that it was so good for me. There were fresh juices, crunchy salads and thirst-quenching coconut water. Yum! Breakfast was the highlight, providing an array of tropical fruits and interesting Asian breakfasts, but I couldn't go past the bircher muesli with all the delicious additions on offer, such as roasted nuts, seeds, dried fruit and organic yoghurt. I have this now at home regularly—it is so easy to make and it's a great start to the day.

Combine the oats, LSA mix, milk, apple juice, lemon juice and, if you like, apricot kernels, in a large bowl, cover with plastic wrap and refrigerate overnight.

Mix the grated apple through the oat mixture, then divide the muesli among four bowls.

Add the banana, berries, walnuts and dried apricots or figs. Drizzle with the honey, sprinkle over some sesame seeds and pepitas, dollop on some yoghurt and top with the mint leaves and honeycomb.

Note: LSA mix is a mixture of equal quantities of ground linseeds, sunflower seeds and almonds. Specialist health-food products, such as LSA and ground apricot kernels can be found at health-food stores and online.

BANANA AND DATE PORRIDGE

250 g (9 oz/2½ cups) quick-cooking rolled (porridge) oats
1½ ripe bananas, diced
100 g (3½ oz) dates, pitted and chopped
500 ml (17 fl oz/2 cups) almond milk or milk
1½ tablespoons organic honey
½ teaspoon ground cinnamon
extra ½ banana, sliced, for garnish
¼ cup raw almonds, toasted and chopped
extra organic honey, to serve

I don't know how many serves of porridge I've made in my lifetime, but let me put it this way ... it's a lot! I have owned restaurants now for just on 20 years, and some of them serve breakfast. Since this is the shift that most chefs don't like to work (as chefs are generally night owls), it has usually been my job to do the morning shift to make sure that the job gets done to my very high standards. This porridge is a terrific breakfast to make at home and one I often serve my children as it is quite healthy, very simple to make, tastes great and keeps the kids full of energy all the way through to lunch time.

Combine the oats, diced banana, dates, milk, honey and cinnamon in a small saucepan and bring to the boil. Reduce to low heat and continue cooking, stirring occasionally, for 5 minutes, or until the oats are soft. If it looks like it needs a splash more liquid, add some more milk so you achieve the consistency you desire.

Serve the porridge warm with extra sliced banana, toasted almonds and a drizzle of extra honey.

GRILLED ASPARAGUS WITH POACHED EGG, GRUYERE AND SERRANO HAM

4 SERVES

2 bunches (400 g/14 oz) asparagus,
    trimmed and cut in half
2 teaspoons white wine vinegar
1 teaspoon salt
4 free-range eggs
40 g (1½ oz) butter
2 teaspoons finely chopped flat-leaf
    (Italian) parsley
juice of 1 lemon
4–8 slices of sourdough bread
150 g (5½ oz) gruyère cheese, shaved
    or grated
8 slices of serrano ham or prosciutto

The bestseller on my breakfast menus has always been my eggs Benedict, with either salmon or ham. Making the hollandaise sauce that goes with this is a bit of an art form and making just a small amount for breakfast can be a bit of a pain. This recipe is my cheat's version for when I want to make it at home and don't feel like getting out the whisk. I still have the eggs and ham (I like the Spanish jamón ibérico or serrano), but I replace the hollandaise with aromatic gruyère cheese and add some delicious freshly grilled asparagus for flavour and texture. If you want to make traditional eggs Benedict, the recipe for salmon eggs benny with salmon caviar is in my *Fish* cookbook.

Preheat the oven to 200°C (400°F/Gas 6). Cook the asparagus in boiling salted water until tender, then drain. Set aside until needed.

Fill a saucepan with water until approximately 10 cm (4 inches) deep. Add the vinegar and salt. Bring to the boil over medium–high heat, then reduce the heat to low–medium so the water starts to simmer. Crack one egg into a cup. Using a wooden spoon or a whisk stir the simmering water in one direction to form a whirlpool. Slide one egg in and cook for 3 minutes or until cooked to your liking. Remove the egg with a slotted spoon and sit on paper towel to soak up the excess water. Repeat with the remaining eggs.

In a frying pan over medium heat, gently heat the butter until melted, then add the parsley, asparagus, lemon juice, and some salt and freshly ground black pepper and cook until the asparagus starts to colour. Remove from the heat.

Meanwhile, toast the sourdough and place on a baking tray.

Divide the asparagus into four portions and put each portion on a piece of toast, then top each with a poached egg. Top this with the gruyère and heat in the oven until the cheese is just melted. Serve with the serrano ham or prosciutto and extra toast, if you like.

BRAISED BEANS WITH BAKED EGGS

6 SERVES

400 g (14 oz/2 cups) dried cannellini beans
3 tablespoons olive oil
6 garlic cloves, sliced
1 small onion, thinly sliced
1 red capsicum (pepper), core removed,
    sliced into 2 cm (¾ inch) strips
1 yellow capsicum (pepper), core removed,
    sliced into 2 cm (¾ inch) strips
8 ripe tomatoes, roughly chopped
750 ml (26 fl oz/3 cups) chicken stock
    (see page 133)
1 small ham hock
1 teaspoon smoked paprika
100 g (3½ oz/2 loosely packed cups) baby
    English spinach leaves
6 free-range eggs
1 handful of flat-leaf (Italian) parsley,
    chopped

I was a fussy child and I think it was because the first things I tried were not of great quality. No, Mum, I'm not having a dig at you, but things were different back then. I remember the first time I tried baked beans they were out of a tin; I still remember the unappetizing flavour. I can't believe that even today people eat them and think that is what baked beans should taste like. It wasn't until I started cooking professionally and was cooking breakfast for customers that I researched baked beans from many different cuisines. What a revelation. Since then I have cooked countless different recipes for baked beans but this one is my favourite and I hope it will be yours, too. I love to crack a couple of eggs into it to make it a complete breakfast and serve it with some toast to mop up all that delicious sauce mixed with the egg yolk. It's definitely not a quick breakfast, but it's worth spending the time on it.

Soak the cannellini beans in water overnight. Rinse and drain.

Heat the oil in a saucepan, then sweat the garlic, onion, capsicums and tomato for about 10 minutes until they begin to soften.

Add the stock, beans, ham hock and paprika and bring to the boil. Reduce the heat and maintain a simmer, stirring occasionally, for 1–1½ hours until the beans are tender.

When the beans are cooked, stir through the spinach, then remove the pan from the heat. Remove any meat from the ham hock, chop and return to the pan. Season with salt. Allow to cool. (This can be done days in advance and the mixture frozen—gently reheat the beans before using.)

Preheat the oven to 200°C (400°F/Gas 6). Spoon 2 large spoonfuls of beans into six shallow ovenproof baking dishes of about 310 ml (10¾ fl oz/1¼ cup) capacity, make a small well in the centre and break in an egg. Bake for 5–10 minutes, or until the egg is cooked to your liking. Remove from the oven, sprinkle with chopped parsley and serve immediately.

MUSHROOMS ON TOAST

4 SERVES

100 g (3½ oz) butter
180 g (6 oz/2 cups) sliced field mushrooms
90 g (3¼ oz/1 cup) mixture of sliced
   shiitake, oyster and button mushrooms
2 garlic cloves, minced
pinch of smoked paprika
400 ml (14 fl oz) cream
3 tablespoons chopped flat-leaf (Italian)
   parsley
8 slices of sourdough bread
extra butter
shaved parmesan, for garnish

This recipe comes from an amazing chef who really loves working with local produce—his name is Steve Cumper and he owns the Red Velvet Lounge in Cygnet, Tasmania. On a recent trip I popped in for breakfast and didn't want anything fancy so I ordered mushrooms on toast and they were the best I have ever had. Here is the recipe. Enjoy!

Melt the butter in a frying pan over medium heat until it sizzles. Add all the mushrooms and the garlic and cook until the mushrooms change colour. Reduce any liquid in the pan. Add the paprika and cream and reduce the cream by one-quarter before adding salt, freshly ground black pepper and parsley.

Meanwhile, toast the bread, then spread with the extra butter.

Put two pieces of toast on each plate, top with the mushrooms, then scatter with parmesan.

BREAKFAST PIZZA WITH PROSCIUTTO, SPINACH, EGG AND TOMATO

4 SERVES

BASIC PIZZA DOUGH

1½ teaspoons dried yeast
1½ teaspoons sugar
½ teaspoon salt
2 teaspoons olive oil
125 ml (4 fl oz/½ cup) warm water
215 g (7½ oz) bakers' flour

pinch of dried oregano
160 g (5¾ oz/⅔ cup) tomato passata (puréed tomatoes)
100 g (3½ oz/⅔ cup) grated pizza cheese
about 5 roma (plum) tomatoes, thinly sliced (you'll need 24 slices of tomato)
160 g (5¾ oz) baby English spinach leaves, blanched in water, refreshed and squeezed dry
12 slices of prosciutto
4 free-range eggs
1 large handful of rocket (arugula)
squeeze of lemon
drizzle of extra virgin olive oil
125 g (4½ oz/½ cup) ricotta
pinch of chilli flakes (optional)

I own a few restaurants that serve pizzas; at all of them we take our pizzas very seriously. We have won the prize for best pizza in Australia a number of times and also World's Best Pizza at the New York Pizza Showcase. I sometimes make these breakfast pizzas at home—they are a lot of fun to make and eat, and you can make the dough in advance and have it rolled out between sheets of baking paper so all you have to do is top them and bake them. A wood-fired oven is the traditional and best way to cook a pizza, but the next best thing is one of the small domestic pizza ovens that do a wonderful job, too.

To make the dough, put the yeast, sugar, salt and olive oil in a bowl with the warm water and stir gently. Leave for 15 minutes for the yeast to activate (it will look foamy).

Slowly add the flour and knead for about 5 minutes until the dough is smooth. Put the dough in a lightly oiled bowl and leave in a warm place for between 30 minutes and 1 hour until doubled in size, then knock back with one good punch. Leave in a warm place until it has risen slightly.

Preheat the oven to 230°C (450°F/Gas 8). Divide the dough into four pieces. Roll out each portion of pizza dough to 15 cm (6 inches) in diameter on a piece of baking paper, lay on a 15 cm (6 inch) pizza tray and prick the bases all over with a fork to stop air bubbles forming when cooking.

Mix the oregano with the passata, season with salt and freshly ground black pepper and spread out over the pizza bases. Sprinkle the cheese evenly over the bases, then top with the sliced tomatoes, spinach and prosciutto. Crack 1 egg onto each pizza then bake for up to 10 minutes.

Place the rocket in a bowl, add the lemon juice, olive oil and salt and freshly ground black pepper, then mix well.

Arrange the dressed rocket over the pizzas, then sprinkle with the ricotta and, if you like, chilli flakes.

BREAKFAST PRAWN AND CORN QUESADILLAS

4 SERVES

1 corn cob, husk removed
1 teaspoon chilli flakes
2 garlic cloves, minced
juice and zest of 2 limes
2 tablespoons olive oil
350 g (12 oz) prawns (shrimp), peeled and deveined, tails removed
1 small bunch of coriander (cilantro), chopped
16 cherry tomatoes, cut into quarters
1 avocado, sliced and sprinkled with lime juice
1 red onion, thinly sliced
150 g (5½ oz) manchego cheese, grated
8 flour or corn tortillas
125 g (4½ oz/½ cup) crème fraîche or sour cream
Mexican chilli sauce (optional)

I love the idea of a Mexican-style breakfast but I would like to think it doesn't have to be as heavy and fattening as the infamous breakfast burrito that is served throughout the USA. A beautiful seafood-focused Mexican breakfast like this hits the mark for me—it is quick, tasty, can be shared with friends and won't weigh you down.

Preheat a barbecue hotplate or grill (broiler) to medium (or heat a frying pan over medium heat). While the barbecue is heating, cook the corn in boiling salted water until tender. Drain, then transfer the corn to the barbecue, grill or frying pan and cook for 10 minutes, turning occasionally, until blackened in places. Cool slightly, then remove the kernels from the cob with a knife.

Combine the chilli flakes, garlic, lime zest and juice, oil and a pinch of salt in a large bowl. Divide the mixture among two bowls.

Add the prawns to one bowl and stir to coat well with the mixture. Barbecue or pan-fry the prawns for 2–3 minutes on each side until just cooked through. Roughly chop the prawns, then add the chopped prawns and corn kernels to the second bowl of lime seasoning mixture along with the tomato, avocado, onion and grated cheese. Toss together.

Heat four of the tortillas on the barbecue, grill or frying pan. Top the tortillas with some of the prawn mixture, then add a second tortilla as a 'lid' and cook until the tortilla is toasted and the cheese has melted. Turn once and cook the second side briefly. Serve with crème fraîche or sour cream and some chilli sauce, if you like.

LAP CHEONG AND EGG CONGEE, MY WAY

4 SERVES

740 g (1 lb 10 oz/4 cups) cooked long-grain white rice
2.5 litres (10 cups) chicken stock (see page 133)
65 g (2¼ oz/⅓ cup) thinly sliced fresh ginger
vegetable oil
4 Chinese sausages (lap cheong), sliced, or 2 slices of bacon, sliced (see Note)
1 handful of roughly chopped coriander (cilantro)
50 g (1¾ oz/¾ cup) thinly sliced spring onion (scallion), white and green part
4 bird's eye chillies, thinly sliced
80 ml (2½ fl oz/⅓ cup) soy sauce
ground white pepper and sea salt
4 free-range eggs
toasted sesame seeds, for garnish
sesame oil, for garnish (optional)

If you look at breakfasts from around the world, hardly any include milk, cereal or bread—breakfast is more likely to be a broth that is served with rice or noodles and sometimes some protein. I think this is a wonderful way to start the day as I am not a fan of the Western breakfast because it is generally so high in sugar or made with highly processed foods. Give this congee a try—you can speed up the process by using some leftover rice from the night before and, if you're like me, you'll have some small containers of frozen chicken stock waiting in the freezer to pull out for a dish such as this.

Place the rice, stock and ginger in a large saucepan and bring to the boil. Reduce to a simmer and cook for 30 minutes, or until the rice starts to soften and break down.

Meanwhile, heat a frying pan with a little oil and fry the sausage or bacon until just starting to become crisp, then remove and reserve.

When the rice is lovely and soupy, add the sausage and coriander, spring onion, chilli and soy sauce. Season with white pepper and sea salt. Return to the boil. Divide among four bowls and crack an egg into the centre of each one. Allow to stand for 3–5 minutes so the heat of the congee will cook the eggs. Sprinkle with sesame seeds and drizzle with sesame oil, if you like.

Note: Lap cheong are dried Chinese pork sausages available vacuum-packed at select supermarkets and Asian food stores.

VIETNAMESE PHO

6 SERVES

BROTH

1 piece cassia bark or 1 cinnamon stick
1 tablespoon coriander seeds
1 tablespoon fennel seeds
4 star anise
3 cardamom pods
5 whole cloves
2 onions, peeled and halved
3 tablespoons sliced fresh ginger
vegetable oil
5 litres (20 cups) water
400 g (14 oz) oxtail or other beef bones,
    cut into 5 cm (2 inch) pieces
800 g (1 lb 12 oz) gravy beef, such as flank
1½ tablespoons sea salt
70 ml (2¼ fl oz) fish sauce
2.5 cm (1 inch) chunk of yellow rock sugar
    or white sugar (about 50 g/1¾ oz)

TO SERVE

300 g (10½ oz) thick fresh or dried
    rice noodles
200 g (7 oz) eye fillet or sirloin beef
    (wagyu, if possible), sliced
100 g (3½ oz) bean sprouts, trimmed
1 large handful each of mint, coriander
    (cilantro), Thai basil and sliced spring
    onion (scallion)
80 ml (2½ fl oz/⅓ cup) hoisin sauce
Sriracha hot chilli sauce (optional)
2–3 bird's eye chillies, thinly sliced
2 limes, cut into wedges

I have included this recipe in the breakfast section as that is when pho is generally eaten in Vietnam but it is just as good at any time of the day: brekky, lunch or dinner. Pho is a meal in itself—you won't need anything else if you have this. I travelled through Vietnam recently and I ate this dish nearly every day and each time it was different. The main thing to remember here is that this dish is all about the broth, so take the time to make it properly. You can also freeze the broth so make a big batch so you don't have to do it again for a while. Enjoy the beautiful flavours of Vietnam.

To make the broth, wrap the spices in a piece of muslin (cheesecloth) and secure with string so you have a little flavour bag.

In a large stockpot, cook off the onion and ginger in a touch of oil until they get a bit of colour; once coloured, add the water, bones, gravy beef and flavour bag and simmer for 2–3 hours, frequently skimming any scum from the surface. Once the beef is tender, season the broth with the salt, fish sauce and sugar. Allow to cool, then strain into a large bowl, reserving the beef.

Once the meat is cool enough to handle, remove the oxtail meat from the bones and dice the flesh; shred the gravy meat and place both in a bowl.

Return the broth to the pot and return to the boil. If you are using fresh noodles, blanch them for 20 seconds, then drain. If you are using dried noodles, cook in boiling water for 2–3 minutes, or until just tender, then drain. Fill each serving bowl with some rice noodles, cooked and raw beef, then top with the boiling broth, sprouts, herbs and sauces. Top with chilli and serve lime wedges on the side.

GRAPEFRUIT, MINT AND PEAR JUICE

1 SERVE

80 ml (2½ fl oz/⅓ cup) ruby red
    grapefruit juice
50 ml (1½ fl oz) grapefruit juice
½ pear, core removed, peeled and
    chopped
6 mint leaves
piece of pear and/or a sprig of mint,
    for garnish (optional)

What could be better than coming home from a run or a surf and making a fresh juice using whatever fruit is at its absolute peak for the season? Or a delicious summer smoothie of mango, banana, honey, yoghurt and cinnamon? I often make fresh juices and smoothies instead of eating a sit-down breakfast to keep me going until lunch time—it's a great way to lose weight and to break the habit of eating either a big breakfast or the same old thing day after day. The variety is endless and, better still, delicious.

Place all the ingredients in a blender. Blend thoroughly then strain into a highball glass over ice. Garnish with a slice of pear and/or a sprig of mint, if you like.

PINEAPPLE, APPLE AND GINGER JUICE

1 SERVE

½ pineapple, core removed, sliced
1 apple, core removed, sliced
25 ml (1 fl oz) cranberry juice
2 thin slices of fresh ginger
fresh fruit slices, for garnish (optional)

Place all the ingredients in a blender. Blend thoroughly then strain into a highball glass over ice. Garnish with slices of fruit, if you like.

SPICED HONEY SMOOTHIE

1 SERVE

2 bananas, thinly sliced
3 large slices of mango
6 ice cubes
1 tablespoon organic honey
100 g (3½ oz) plain yoghurt
1 tablespoon milk
pinch of ground cinnamon
ground almonds, for garnish (optional)
sliced dried apricots, for garnish (optional)

Place the banana, mango, ice cubes, honey, yoghurt, milk and cinnamon in a blender. Blend thoroughly then strain into a highball glass. Garnish with ground almonds and slices of dried apricots, if you like.

MANGO AND BERRY SMOOTHIE

1 SERVE

½ mango, peeled and chopped
½ peach, peeled and chopped
6 blueberries (optional)
6 raspberries
100 g (3½ oz) plain yoghurt
½ teaspoon white sugar
6 ice cubes
assorted berries, for garnish (optional)

Place all the ingredients in a blender. Blend thoroughly then strain into a highball glass. Garnish with berries, if you like.

LUNCH & DINNER

02

VEGETARIAN

SPINACH AND LENTIL CURRY WITH CHICKPEAS AND BOILED EGG

RAITA

1 Lebanese (short) cucumber
250 g (9 oz/1 cup) thick plain yoghurt
1 teaspoon ground cumin
2 tablespoons finely chopped mint

300 g (10½ oz/1½ cups) yellow lentils
about 1 litre (4 cups) water
2 x 400 g (14 oz) tins chickpeas, rinsed
   and drained
6 small potatoes, diced
2 tablespoons sunflower oil or ghee
2 large garlic cloves, minced
2 cm (¾ inch) knob of fresh ginger,
   peeled and finely chopped
large pinch of yellow mustard seeds
large pinch of cumin seeds
large pinch of ground cumin
large pinch of ground coriander
200 g (7 oz/4 cups) baby English
   spinach leaves
3 tablespoons coriander (cilantro) leaves
juice of ½ lemon
4 hard-boiled free-range eggs, cut
   into quarters

I am a firm believer that we don't have to consume meat as part of every meal; I think that if we have a diet rich in fruit, vegetables, legumes and seafood, and eat only small quantities of meat we would all be a lot healthier. This doesn't mean I don't eat meat—I love it—but I don't eat it every day of the week. In fact, a lot of my diet is seafood and vegetarian. I enjoy coming up with new vegetarian dishes that are simple, flavoursome and nutritious, such as this one. I usually serve this with brown rice because I love the flavour and texture, but it is equally good with white rice, though not as nutritious.

To make the raita, cut the cucumber in half lengthways and use a teaspoon to scrape out the seeds; coarsely grate the flesh. Squeeze out the excess liquid using your hand. Combine the cucumber flesh with the yoghurt, cumin, mint and some salt in a bowl; stir well to combine. Season to taste.

Rinse the lentils and add to a saucepan with the water. Bring to the boil, then turn down to a simmer and simmer for 15 minutes before adding the chickpeas and diced potato. Simmer for an additional 10 minutes, or until the potato is tender. Drain, then transfer to a large bowl.

Meanwhile, heat the oil or ghee in a small saucepan. Toast the garlic, ginger, mustard seeds and cumin seeds for 1 minute. Add the ground cumin and coriander. Cook for another minute then turn off the heat.

In a food processor, blend the spinach, fresh coriander and a pinch of salt and freshly ground black pepper until puréed.

Add the toasted spices, puréed spinach, lemon juice and some sea salt to the drained lentils and chickpeas, then mix well. Serve with the egg and raita on top.

4-6 SERVES

60 g (2¼ oz) butter
3 tablespoons organic honey
65 g (2¼ oz/½ cup) slivered almonds, toasted
3 tablespoons white wine vinegar
1 tablespoon orange blossom water
juice of 2 lemons
1 red chilli, seeds removed and thinly sliced
150 ml (5 fl oz) extra virgin olive oil
25 red, purple, white and yellow baby carrots, peeled and trimmed
250 g (9 oz/1 cup) plain yoghurt
lamb's lettuce (corn salad), to serve

BABY CARROT SALAD

I am a huge fan of salads—they can make for a spectacular lunch, a stunning first course or an interesting side dish. The pure simplicity of this dish is what makes it so appealing— some gorgeous baby carrots simply boiled and tossed in an aromatic dressing with toasted almonds, fresh herbs and top-quality yoghurt. The recipe was taught to me by a wonderful chef, Matt Wilkinson. I was in Melbourne doing some filming for my TV series and Matt took me to see his wonderful organic vegetable garden in St Kilda.

Put the butter in a saucepan over medium-high heat and cook until the butter turns nut brown. Add the honey to stop the butter cooking, then add the toasted almonds.

Bring the butter and honey back to the boil and let it reduce for 1 minute, then add the vinegar, orange blossom water and lemon juice. Bring back to the boil again and allow to boil for 2 minutes. Take off the heat and add the chilli and oil and mix thoroughly. Leave at room temperature to cool.

Place the carrots into a saucepan of salted water and bring to the boil. Turn down to a simmer and cook for 8 minutes; test the carrots with a sharp knife to see if they are cooked, then drain. While the carrots are still hot, cut them into halves lengthways, place into a bowl and toss in 80 ml (2½ fl oz/⅓ cup) of the honey dressing.

Divide the carrots among each serving plate, top with some lamb's lettuce, then serve with the yoghurt and remaining dressing.

WARM ASPARAGUS SALAD WITH BUFFALO MOZZARELLA AND CHERRY TOMATOES

4 SERVES

20 green asparagus spears
150 ml (5 fl oz) extra virgin olive oil
6 garlic cloves, sliced
14 cherry tomatoes, cut in half
15 black olives, pitted and cut in half
juice of 2 lemons
1 handful of flat-leaf (Italian) parsley,
   chopped
2 buffalo mozzarella, cut in half
pinch of chilli flakes
2 tablespoons baby purple basil

We have been serving this dish in our restaurants for the last few years and it is also one I never get tired of cooking at home when I have friends over. It has everything I like in a dish—it is quick, simple, tasty and quite good for you. It really makes a lovely lunch or starter. If you want to make it into more of a meal, then toast some sourdough, break it into pieces and mix with the tomatoes, or simply toss some cooked pasta through the salad.

Blanch the asparagus in boiling water for 2 minutes, then refresh in iced water until the asparagus is cold. Remove from the water and place on paper towel to soak up the excess water.

In a frying pan, heat the olive oil over medium heat, add the garlic and cook until light golden. Add the cherry tomatoes, olives, lemon juice and parsley and cook for 30 seconds, then toss in the asparagus and cook for a further 30 seconds. Season with salt and freshly ground black pepper.

Arrange the asparagus salad on four plates. Top with the mozzarella, then sprinkle with chilli flakes and baby purple basil.

WARM BABY BEETROOT, GOAT'S CHEESE AND WALNUT SALAD

4–6 SERVES

2 bunches of baby red and gold beetroot
  (beets), about 20
½ bunch of thyme
2 tablespoons olive oil
100 g (3½ oz/1 cup) walnuts
extra 80 ml (2½ fl oz/⅓ cup) olive oil
2 tablespoons good-quality red wine
  vinegar
2 teaspoons lemon juice
200 g (7 oz) goat's chèvre
1 bunch of chives, cut into 5 cm (2 inch)
  lengths

Growing up, the two things I couldn't stand to eat were asparagus and beetroot. Like a lot of Aussies, my first introduction to the humble beetroot was through my love of hamburgers and steak sandwiches and, unfortunately, the beetroot in these would come out of a tin. My aversion to all beetroot stemmed from the taste of the tinned variety, in the same way that tinned asparagus turned me off fresh. It wasn't until I started working in a professional kitchen that I got to taste my first roasted beetroot ... what a difference! Now I love beetroot however it is prepared—roasted, puréed or pickled—and I particularly love this salad, which features beetroot as the star ingredient. And these days I don't mind the odd slice of tinned beetroot on my burgers.

Preheat the oven to 180°C (350°F/Gas 4). Trim the beetroot stems, leaving 1 cm (½ inch) intact. Wash the beetroot, place in a baking dish, then sprinkle with thyme, oil, salt and freshly ground black pepper. Tightly cover the dish with foil and roast the beetroot for about 40 minutes, or until tender, shaking the pan after 20 minutes. Remove the beetroot from the dish. When cool enough to touch, peel off the skin.

Meanwhile, place the walnuts on a baking tray. Bake for about 5 minutes or until toasted. Coarsely chop.

Combine the extra oil, vinegar, lemon juice and half the walnuts in a small screw-top jar with a little salt and freshly ground black pepper. Shake well.

Cut some of the larger beetroot in half lengthways, but leave the smaller beetroot whole, if you prefer.

Thickly spread the goat's chèvre out on a large platter and top with the warm beetroot. Drizzle the beetroot with the dressing, then scatter over the chives and season with salt and freshly ground black pepper. Garnish with the remaining walnuts. Serve warm.

NOODLE SALAD WITH HERBS AND TOASTED PEANUTS

4 SERVES

DRESSING

2 tablespoons sweet chilli sauce
2 tablespoons light soy sauce
1½ tablespoons sesame oil
3 tablespoons lime juice
1 tablespoon sugar
1 tablespoon seeded and finely diced
   long red chilli
1 tablespoon kecap manis
80 ml (2½ fl oz/⅓ cup) grapeseed oil

300 g (10½ oz) thin hokkien noodles
125 ml (4 fl oz/½ cup) grapeseed oil
280 g (10 oz) mixed Asian mushrooms
   (such as oyster, shiitake and wood ear),
   thinly sliced
150 g (5½ oz) Chinese cabbage, shredded
80 g (2¾ oz) red Asian shallots, thinly
   sliced
2 teaspoons black sesame seeds
2 teaspoons white sesame seeds, toasted
2 large handfuls of mixed picked Asian
   herbs (such as Thai basil, Vietnamese
   mint and coriander/cilantro)
4 spring onions (scallions), thinly sliced
80 g (2¾ oz/½ cup) crisp-fried onion
   or shallots
60 g (2¼ oz) toasted salted peanuts,
   roughly chopped
extra toasted sesame seeds, for garnish

In the warmer months I love making flavour-filled salads that don't rely on the old lettuce, cucumber and tomato scenario. Noodle salads are very impressive as they are something everyone can appreciate, from youngsters to the sophisticated palates of the older generations. You can have a lot of fun playing around with noodle salads and, once you have decided on your region of choice, find a suitable dressing in keeping with that cuisine and then top it up with whatever is in season that you love to eat. This recipe is from Matt Drummond, a great chef who has been working with me for the past 11 years.

To make the dressing, mix all the ingredients together and set aside.

Place the hokkien noodles in a heatproof bowl and cover with boiling water. Gently separate the noodles. Drain. Mix one-third of the dressing with the noodles.

Heat a wok or large frying pan over medium–high heat and add 1 tablespoon of the grapeseed oil. Add the noodles and sauté for 2–3 minutes, then remove from the pan and set aside in a large bowl.

Using another pan, heat 100 ml (3½ fl oz) of the grapeseed oil and sauté all the mushrooms for 3–4 minutes, or until they are golden, then add the cabbage and shallots and sauté for a further minute. Remove from the pan and place in the bowl with the noodles. Add the sesame seeds and remaining dressing to the bowl and mix together. Gently mix in the herbs and spring onion.

Divide the salad among four bowls or arrange on one large dish and garnish with the crisp-fried shallots, chopped peanuts and extra toasted sesame seeds.

Note: This salad can be served cold, warm or hot.

POTATO AND RICOTTA RAVIOLI WITH BLACK TRUFFLE

4–6 SERVES

FILLING

250 g (9 oz) desiree potatoes, peeled
250 g (9 oz) fresh ricotta
100 g (3½ oz/¾ cup) freshly grated
   parmesan
1 tablespoon finely chopped mint

400 g (14 oz/2⅔ cups) plain (all-purpose)
   flour (preferably '00')
3 free-range eggs
approximately 2 tablespoons water
250 g (9 oz) butter
50 g (1¾ oz/1 cup) coarsely chopped mint
8 thin slices of black truffle, for garnish
   (optional)

This recipe was inspired by my good friend and chef Giovanni Pilu. I added sliced truffle to the dish though a good substitute that won't break the bank is truffle-infused pecorino cheese.

To make the filling, place the potato in a saucepan of cold, salted water. Bring to the boil. Boil gently until tender. Drain well, then mash with a potato masher. Cool for 5 minutes, then stir in the ricotta, parmesan and mint. Season with salt and freshly ground black pepper.

Sift the flour and a little salt onto a clean workbench. Make a well in the centre. Add the eggs and whisk lightly with a fork. Add a little of the water. Using your hands, gradually incorporate the flour into the centre, adding enough of the remaining water to form a soft pliable dough. The dough is the correct consistency if your thumb comes back clean when pushed into it.

Knead the dough on a lightly floured workbench for about 5 minutes or until smooth and elastic (it will lose its rough, floury texture). Cut into four portions (this will make the rolling process more manageable). Pass a portion of dough through a pasta machine on the widest setting, repeating on all but the last setting. Lay the thin pasta sheet on a workbench, then repeat.

Place rounded teaspoons of filling onto one of the pasta sheets about 7 cm (2¾ inches) apart, leaving a 2 cm (¾ inch) border. Brush with a little water in between mounds of filling. Top with a second pasta sheet and press the edges together to seal. Cut between the filling using a sharp knife or cookie cutter, to form squares or rounds. Repeat with the remaining pasta sheets and filling.

Cook the ravioli in batches, in a large saucepan of boiling salted water until al dente. Remove with a slotted spoon.

To make the sauce, melt the butter in a large frying pan over low heat. Stir in the mint. Season. Add the ravioli, then toss to combine. Divide among serving plates, then garnish with truffle slices, if using.

Note: For a lighter filling, bake the potatoes until tender. Scoop out the flesh, then combine with the remaining ingredients.

CHICKPEA AND SWEET POTATO SALAD WITH YOGHURT DRESSING

4–6 SERVES

220 g (7¾ oz/1 cup) dried chickpeas

1.2 kg (2 lb 10 oz) orange sweet potato, cut into 3 cm (1¼ inch) chunks

2 tablespoons extra virgin olive oil

1 teaspoon sea salt

1 teaspoon cumin seeds

1 red onion, halved and each half cut into six wedges

150 g (5½ oz/3 cups) baby English spinach leaves

150 g (5½ oz/1 cup) pepitas (pumpkin seeds), toasted

YOGHURT DRESSING

300 g (10½ oz) plain yoghurt

1 tablespoon tahini

2 garlic cloves, minced

½ teaspoon sumac

½ teaspoon ground coriander

3 tablespoons lemon juice

This delicious salad is so filling that it can be eaten on its own, or you can serve it as part of a Morrocan or Middle Eastern feast. You can play around with substitutions or additions to this salad with ingredients such as pumpkin (winter squash), zucchini (courgette), green beans and carrots. The keys to this dish are to make sure you cook your vegetables so they are tender, and to ensure you are getting the balance of flavours right in the dressing. This is perfect as an accompaniment to a spiced roast chicken, or a harissa-spiced roasted leg of lamb.

Soak the chickpeas in plenty of water overnight. Rinse and drain. Place in a saucepan and cover well with water, bring to the boil and cook for 45–60 minutes or until the chickpeas are tender. Drain and set aside.

Preheat the oven to 180°C (350°F/Gas 4). Lightly grease a baking tray. Toss the sweet potato with the oil, salt and cumin seeds. Place the sweet potato on the prepared tray and roast for 10 minutes, then add the red onion wedges and cook for a further 10 minutes, or until golden and cooked through. Allow to cool.

To make the dressing, put all the ingredients in a bowl and whisk until well combined. Set aside.

Once the sweet potato and onion have cooled, place in a bowl and mix in the spinach, chickpeas and pepitas and season with salt and freshly ground black pepper. Gently drizzle with the dressing.

JERUSALEM ARTICHOKE SOUP WITH CROUTONS

4 SERVES

8 Jerusalem artichokes (about 500 g/
    1 lb 2 oz in total)
2 tablespoons lemon juice
1 tablespoon olive oil
2 leeks, white part only, sliced (about
    700 g/1 lb 9 oz in total)
5 garlic cloves, sliced
20 g (¾ oz) unsalted butter
1 potato, coarsely chopped (about
    200 g/7 oz)
1.5 litres (6 cups) vegetable or chicken
    stock (see page 133)
170 ml (5½ fl oz/⅔ cup) cream
1 handful of flat-leaf (Italian) parsley,
    chopped
extra olive oil, for garnish

CROUTONS

½ loaf of 1-day-old sourdough bread
3 tablespoons olive oil
100 g (3½ oz) unsalted butter, cut into
    cubes
5 garlic cloves, minced

In my eyes, Jerusalem artichokes are one of the darlings of the vegetable world. As they aren't always available, I urge you to buy them whenever you see them. They are amazing when roasted in their skins and served with a dollop of good-quality crème fraîche with one of your favourite roasts; cooked Jerusalem artichokes also purée beautifully. Here they make a wonderful soup served with some simple croutons, again with a dollop of crème fraîche if you're feeling a little indulgent.

Peel the artichokes, then chop into 1 cm (½ inch) pieces. Place the chopped artichoke in a bowl of cold water with the lemon juice until ready—the lemon juice will prevent the artichoke from discolouring.

Heat the oil in a heavy-based saucepan over medium heat, add the leek and garlic and cook for 5 minutes. Add the butter and cook for a further 10 minutes, stirring constantly, until the leek is soft but not coloured. Add the drained artichokes, potato and stock and bring to the boil. Simmer, covered, for about 40 minutes or until the vegetables are soft, stirring occasionally. Cool for 10 minutes.

Blend or process the soup until smooth. Add the cream and season to taste with salt and freshly ground black pepper. Reheat the soup if necessary.

Meanwhile, to make the croutons, remove the crusts from the bread and cut the bread into 1.5 cm (⅝ inch) thick slices. Cut each slice into 1.5 cm (⅝ inch) strips, then cut each strip into small squares. Heat the oil in a large frying pan over medium heat, then add the butter and garlic. Once the butter melts, add the bread cubes. Cook, stirring often and watching carefully as they can burn quickly, until golden brown. Remove with a slotted spoon and drain on paper towel. Sprinkle with salt.

Ladle the soup into warm bowls, then top with the croutons and some parsley and drizzle with a little olive oil.

PAPPARDELLE WITH SILVERBEET, PINE NUTS AND GOAT'S CHEESE

125 ml (4 fl oz/½ cup) olive oil
4 garlic cloves, chopped
1 large onion, diced
300 g (10½ oz) silverbeet (Swiss chard) leaves, shredded
80 ml (2½ fl oz/⅓ cup) water
400 g (14 oz) fresh pappardelle (see Notes)
⅓ cup chopped flat-leaf (Italian) parsley
50 g (1¾ oz/⅓ cup) pine nuts, toasted
125 ml (4 fl oz/½ cup) extra virgin olive oil
100 g (3½ oz) fresh goat's cheese or goat's curd (see Notes)
juice and zest of 1 lemon
2 pinches of chilli flakes (optional)

I love a dish like this one where there are only a few good-quality ingredients. This is a wonderful meal that is perfect for lunch or dinner when you don't want to spend too much time in the kitchen. It is also a great way of eating one of my favourite ingredients, silverbeet. If you prefer, you can substitute cavolo nero, English spinach or broccolini for the silverbeet.

Heat the olive oil in a frying pan, add the garlic and cook until lightly golden, then add the onion and cook for a further 3 minutes or until tender. Add the silverbeet and water and cook for a further 3 minutes, or until the silverbeet is wilted and tender. Season with a good amount of salt and freshly ground black pepper to taste.

Meanwhile, cook the pappardelle in a large saucepan of boiling water until al dente. Drain.

Add the cooked pappardelle to the frying pan with the silverbeet, then add the parsley, pine nuts and extra virgin olive oil and toss until combined.

Divide among four dishes and add a spoonful of goat's cheese to the top of each serving, then add some grated lemon zest, a squeeze of lemon juice, chilli flakes, if using, and some freshly ground black pepper.

Note: If you are unable to find fresh pappardelle, you could use dried. You could use ricotta, blue cheese or buffalo mozzarella instead of the goat's cheese.

PUMPKIN AND BORLOTTI BEAN RISOTTO

4 SERVES

RISOTTO

1 tablespoon olive oil
½ celery stalk, finely diced
¼ red onion, finely diced
1 tablespoon dried oregano
½ teaspoon chilli flakes
1 cinnamon stick
200 g (7 oz) arborio rice
600 ml (21 fl oz) hot vegetable stock,
    plus extra

PUMPKIN

400 g (14 oz) pumpkin (winter squash),
    peeled, seeds removed and cut into 2 cm
    (¾ inch) dice
1 teaspoon dried oregano
2 tablespoons olive oil

3 tablespoons ready-made pasta sauce
30 g (1 oz) butter
100 g (3½ oz) tinned borlotti beans, rinsed
70 g (2½ oz/½ cup) freshly grated
    parmesan
1 vine-ripened tomato, seeds removed
    and diced
1 tablespoon lemon juice
3 tablespoons extra virgin olive oil
1 small handful of basil leaves

As well as being a warming meal for a winter lunch or dinner, risotto also makes a great dish to serve at a party once all the finger food has been consumed. A large pot of risotto will be enough for many small bowls and it will leave your guests feeling satisfied. Choose your favourite risotto recipe and the one you are most confident and proud of serving. This is one of my favourite risottos as it is full of flavour and colour.

Preheat the oven to 180°C (350°F/Gas 4). To make the risotto, heat the oil in a saucepan over medium heat. Add the celery, onion, oregano, chilli and cinnamon stick and cook until the celery and onion are soft but not coloured. Add the rice and stir well so the rice gets coated in the oil, then add the stock. Bring to the boil then turn down to a simmer, stirring continuously, until the liquid has almost evaporated and the rice is cooked. Remove from the stovetop.

Meanwhile, place the pumpkin on a roasting tray and sprinkle with the oregano and some salt and freshly ground black pepper, then drizzle with the oil. Roast for 10-15 minutes, or until soft.

Once the pumpkin is tender, mash it using a potato masher. Add the pumpkin to the risotto and return the risotto to the stovetop over low-medium heat. Stir well. Add the pasta sauce and butter and stir until combined, adding extra stock if needed. Add the borlotti beans and stir well. Season.

To finish, place a good portion of risotto on a plate or serving dish, top with grated parmesan and garnish with diced tomato mixed with the lemon juice, oil and basil.

AGLIO E OLIO PASTA WITH POOR MAN'S PARMESAN AND ZUCCHINI FLOWERS

4 SERVES

POOR MAN'S PARMESAN
25 g (1 oz/⅓ cup) fresh breadcrumbs
zest of 2 lemons
1 tablespoon minced garlic
2 tablespoons chopped flat-leaf (Italian) parsley
2 tablespoons olive oil

500 g (1 lb 2 oz) spaghetti
200 ml (7 fl oz) extra virgin olive oil
6 garlic cloves, chopped
4 anchovies, chopped (optional)
1 teaspoon chilli flakes
⅓ cup finely chopped flat-leaf (Italian) parsley
8 baby zucchini (courgettes) with flowers, cut in half and stamens removed
extra flat-leaf (Italian) parsley leaves, to serve

Aglio e olio is known as the college meal in Italy, as pasta with garlic and oil is one of the cheapest dinners a student can cook. That said, I believe it is also one of the best recipes in the world. The wonderful thing about this dish is that you will have most of the ingredients in your pantry and fridge: pasta, olive oil, garlic, chilli flakes and parsley. I like to serve this with some toasted breadcrumbs or *pangrattato* (poor man's parmesan) on top to give it a bit of crunch but you could simply add some toasted pine nuts for a similar effect.

To make the poor man's parmesan, preheat the oven to 150°C (300°F/ Gas 2). Line a baking tray with baking paper. Mix the breadcrumbs, lemon zest, garlic, parsley and olive oil together, then spread over the prepared baking tray and bake for 10 minutes, or until dry. Grind with a mortar and pestle, leaving the mixture a little coarse.

Cook the spaghetti in a large saucepan of boiling salted water until al dente. Drain.

Meanwhile, to make the sauce, heat the oil in a saucepan over low-medium heat and cook the garlic and anchovies, if using, for 2 minutes. When the garlic starts to colour, add the chilli and parsley and cook for a further 1-2 minutes, or until the garlic starts to lightly colour. Add the zucchini and flowers and cook for 2 minutes.

Add the spaghetti to the sauce and season with salt and freshly ground black pepper; top with the poor man's parmesan and extra parsley leaves.

SEAFOOD

SPANISH BREAD SALAD

4–6 SERVES

4 red capsicums (peppers)
4 vine-ripened tomatoes, cut into quarters
1 loaf of sourdough bread
6 garlic cloves, halved
50 ml (1½ fl oz) extra virgin olive oil
4 white anchovies, torn (optional)
20 black olives
1 tablespoon salted capers, rinsed and
    drained
1 large handful of flat-leaf (Italian)
    parsley leaves
150 g (5½ oz) feta, crumbled

VINAIGRETTE

150 ml (5 fl oz) extra virgin olive oil
    (I like Spanish)
80 ml (2½ fl oz/⅓ cup) sherry vinegar

Over the past 10 years, the accessibility of great bread in towns and suburbs around Australia has increased dramatically. Now we can easily buy a loaf of sourdough or ciabatta bread to make wonderful bruschetta or panini. But what to do when the bread goes stale? Well, this recipe is one great way of using up that stale bread.

Preheat the oven to 200°C (400°F/Gas 6). Place the capsicums on a baking tray and cook for 30–40 minutes or until blackened. Place in a bowl, cover with plastic wrap and allow to cool slightly. Peel and discard the skin and cut the flesh into large strips.

Meanwhile, place the tomatoes on a baking tray and cook for 20–30 minutes, or until lightly roasted. Once both the capsicums and tomatoes are removed from the oven, reduce the oven temperature to 160°C (315°F/Gas 2–3).

Tear the bread into rustic pieces (leaving the crust on) that are just bigger than mouth-size. Rub with the garlic cloves, drizzle liberally with olive oil and season with salt and freshly ground black pepper. Bake for 10 minutes, then mix well and return to the oven until the bread is toasted and golden brown.

Meanwhile, make the vinaigrette by mixing the olive oil with the sherry vinegar.

Soak the baked bread in the vinaigrette for 10 minutes.

Just before you are ready to serve, mix the bread with the capsicum, tomatoes, white anchovies, if using, olives, capers and parsley and season well. Place in a large serving bowl, then fold in most of the feta. Top with the rest of the feta.

OCEAN TROUT IN FOIL WITH MUSSELS AND LEMON BUTTER

4 SERVES

4 x 180 g (6 oz) ocean trout fillets, skinless
2 carrots, julienned
1 leek, white part only, julienned
16 black mussels, scrubbed and beards removed
juice of 1 lemon
40 g (1½ oz) butter
2 tablespoons vermouth
100 ml (3½ fl oz) fish stock
½ bunch of tarragon

You have to love a dish that you can prepare beforehand and then pop in the oven for 10 minutes when it's time to serve. I cook 'fish in the bag' a lot at home as it is extremely easy, not messy and, better still, results in flesh that comes out succulent, moist and full of flavour. Play around with different flavourings to complement your fish, and you can always throw a few mussels or clams in as well to make it more interesting, like I've done here.

Preheat the oven to 180°C (350°F/Gas 4). Cut out four pieces of foil large enough to enclose a trout fillet and 4 mussels; lay the foil pieces on a workbench and top each one with a piece of baking paper the same size.

Divide the julienned carrot and leek among the pieces of foil/paper, then lay a fish fillet on top of each pile. Place 4 mussels on top of each piece of fish and add a squeeze of lemon, 10 g (¼ oz) butter, 2 teaspoons vermouth, 25 ml (1 fl oz) fish stock and a sprig of tarragon to each parcel. Season with salt and freshly ground black pepper. Wrap the foil tightly around the fish and seal.

Place the parcels on a baking tray and bake for 6–10 minutes or until the fish is cooked to medium and the mussels have opened.

Serve the packets on a plate on the table and allow each person to open their sealed fish. Serve with steamed potatoes.

ANGEL HAIR PASTA WITH TUNA, CHILLI, ROCKET AND CAPERS

4 SERVES

DRESSING

125 ml (4 fl oz/½ cup) extra virgin olive oil
2 tablespoons chilli oil
1 garlic clove, minced
125 ml (4 fl oz/½ cup) lemon juice

500 g (1 lb 2 oz) angel hair pasta
400 g (14 oz) tuna loin, cut into 5 cm
  (2 inch) pieces and sliced 5 mm (¼ inch)
  thick
2 long red chillies, seeds removed and
  thinly sliced
3 tablespoons salted baby capers, rinsed
  and drained
3 tablespoons very finely grated parmesan
100 g (3½ oz) rocket (arugula) or 2 large
  handfuls
lemon wedges, to serve

I love, love, love this recipe. In the time it takes to cook the pasta, you will have everything else completed. If your kids love sushi and raw fish then this is a wonderful dish to get them onto so that the whole family can eat the same meal together. The thing to remember here is that the tuna is to stay rare—if you overcook it you may as well be putting in tinned tuna. Just place all the ingredients into a large bowl then add the cooked pasta and that will be enough heat to warm the tuna through.

To make the dressing, whisk together the olive oil, chilli oil, garlic and lemon juice and season with salt and freshly ground black pepper. Set aside.

Cook the pasta in a large saucepan of boiling salted water until al dente. Drain.

Meanwhile, place the tuna, chilli, capers, parmesan and rocket in a bowl ready for the cooked pasta to be tossed through. Once the pasta is ready, toss it in with the tuna salad mixture and pour over the dressing. Gently mix the pasta until combined. Serve immediately with the lemon wedges.

BIBIMBAP SUSHI

4 SERVES

SUSHI RICE
420 g (14¾ oz/2 cups) sushi rice
660 ml (22½ fl oz) water
75 g (2½ oz/⅓ cup) sugar
2 teaspoons sea salt
80 ml (2½ fl oz/⅓ cup) rice vinegar

90 g (3¼ oz/1 cup) bean sprouts, trimmed
3 tablespoons rice vinegar
2 teaspoons salt
1 tablespoon sugar
1 tablespoon soy sauce
pinch of chilli powder
180 g (6 oz) Spanish mackerel or kingfish,
    thinly sliced
180 g (6 oz) bluefin tuna or longtail tuna,
    thinly sliced
180 g (6 oz) trevally, ocean trout or
    Atlantic salmon, thinly sliced
1 Lebanese (short) cucumber, cut in half
    lengthways, seeds scraped out and
    thinly sliced
2 free-range egg yolks
120 g (4¼ oz/½ cup) salmon caviar or
    flying fish roe
3 tablespoons pickled ginger
90 g (3¼ oz/⅓ cup) Japanese mayonnaise
1 tablespoon toasted sesame seeds
2 sheets of toasted Nori (seaweed sheet)
    julienned
tamari and wasabi, to serve

This is a wonderfully easy way to make sushi for the family without having to roll it and cut it into pieces. Make sure you buy the freshest sashimi-grade fish available. For the best result, prepare the rice about 45 minutes before you sit down to eat so it isn't too hot or too cold. If you are not a fan of raw egg, just remember that's what mayonnaise is made of ... you can omit it if you like, but I think it's much better with it.

To make the sushi rice, cook the rice in the water following the packet instructions. Meanwhile, stir the sugar, salt and vinegar in a small saucepan over low heat until the sugar and salt dissolve. Spread the hot cooked rice on a large tray and sprinkle it with the rice vinegar dressing. Stir with chopsticks or a fork to distribute the dressing evenly and cool the rice.

Blanch the bean sprouts in boiling salted water for 30 seconds then refresh under cold water. Combine the vinegar, salt, sugar, soy sauce and chilli powder in a jug, then pour over the cooled bean sprouts to pickle them.

To serve, place the rice in the bottom of a serving dish or platter and top with the fish, bean sprouts, cucumber, egg yolks, caviar or fish roe and pickled ginger. Dot the mayonnaise in a few spots on top of the rice and top with the sesame seeds and nori. Serve with the tamari and wasabi on the side.

Note: Sushi rice is best when not refrigerated and used within 2 hours of making.

GRILLED SKATE WING

4 SERVES

680–900 g (1½–2 lb) whole skate (stingray) wing, cleaned (or other firm flat fish such as sole or flounder), cut into 4 portions
juice of 1 lemon or lime
1 tablespoon tamarind concentrate
250 ml (9 fl oz/1 cup) warm water
8 red Asian shallots, peeled
4 garlic cloves, peeled
2.5 cm (1 inch) knob of fresh ginger, peeled
2 lemongrass stems, white part only, roughly chopped
4–6 dried chillies, softened in hot water
2 tablespoons vegetable oil
1½ teaspoons dried shrimp paste
1½ teaspoons palm sugar (jaggery) or dark brown sugar
2 large pieces of banana leaf or 4 pieces of foil
1 long red chilli, sliced
4 toothpicks, soaked in water
3–4 limes, cut in half
a few sprigs of fresh coriander (cilantro) leaves, for garnish

Whenever I go to Singapore I always pop into the Newton Circus food markets—it's a vibrant place with lots of fresh seafood that you can choose yourself, then watch the chefs cook it for you on the spot. When there I never fail to order the sambal skate (stingray) wing in banana leaf. Sambal isn't 'knock your socks off' hot, but it is very moreish with a great depth of flavour that works with just about any seafood or vegetable and even tofu. My favourite sambal pairing is sambal with skate. Skate is very under-utilised, especially considering that it tastes great, is easy to cook and is also inexpensive.

Rub the skate with lemon or lime juice and some salt, then set aside for 10 minutes.

In a small bowl, mix the tamarind concentrate with the warm water, then strain, discarding the seeds. Set aside.

Using a blender or food processor, process the shallots, garlic, ginger, lemongrass, dried chillies, oil and shrimp paste until it forms a fragrant paste.

Cook the shallot paste in a small heavy-based pan over medium heat for 1–2 minutes or until fragrant. Add the strained tamarind, palm sugar and salt to taste and cook until the sauce is slightly thickened, then allow to cool.

Cut each banana leaf in half, then soften in hot water. Dry well with a kitchen cloth, then lightly coat with some vegetable oil. (If you are using foil, it should also be lightly coated with oil.)

Spoon half the shallot-tamarind sauce evenly among the banana leaves or foil parcels, then spread out evenly. Lay the skate fillets on top, then spoon the rest of the sauce over the fish and top with the sliced chilli. Fold the banana leaves or foil into a packet and secure with the toothpicks. Cook the parcels on a hot charcoal barbecue chargrill, grill (broiler) or chargrill pan for 10–15 minutes, depending on the thickness of the fish, turning over once only. At the same time, cook the lime halves on the grill for 2–3 minutes until lightly charred. Serve the skate parcels with the lime and coriander.

BLACK PEPPER PIPIS

1 kg (2 lb 4 oz) pipis
200 g (7 oz) unsalted butter
6 garlic cloves
1 small knob of fresh ginger, julienned
30 black peppercorns, roughly crushed
1 teaspoon finely chopped coriander
   (cilantro) root
2 long red chillies, seeds removed and
   julienned
2 tablespoons oyster sauce
2 handfuls of snow peas (mangetout),
   sliced on the diagonal
1 cup picked coriander (cilantro) leaves
juice of 1 lemon
lemon wedges, for garnish (optional)

If you like to catch fish, you probably look at pipis and think, 'bait' but in this instance the bait is just as good as the fish you are hoping to catch. I love cooking with pipis, cockles, clams (vongole) and mussels because they can handle strong flavours. Not only that but they are quite inexpensive and a fun option when you have a large group of people around as everyone loves sucking the meat out of the shells. As far as this recipe goes, it works with all of the above-mentioned seafood as well as crab, lobster and prawns (shrimp). So next time you walk past the seafood shop and your eye happens upon those cheap clams or pipis, remember this recipe and give it a go.

Soak the pipis in a bowl of slightly salted cold water for 2 hours to help purge any sand that may be trapped.

Melt half the butter in a wok over medium heat, then sauté the garlic, ginger, pepper, coriander root and chilli until softened and fragrant. Stir in the oyster sauce, then throw in the pipis and keep cooking until they start to open. Once they start to open up, add the remaining butter and stir.

Toss through the snow peas and coriander leaves, lemon juice and add some extra freshly ground black pepper, if needed. Serve on a bed of steamed rice with the lemon wedges.

Note: Don't add any salt to the sauce as the oyster sauce is very salty.

TUNA CROSTINI

4 SERVES

½ baguette, sliced on an angle about
   2 cm (¾ inch) thick
80 ml (2½ fl oz/⅓ cup) extra virgin
   olive oil
400 g (14 oz) tuna, cut into 1 cm
   (½ inch) dice
3 tablespoons lemon-infused olive oil
3 tablespoons chilli oil or 1 tablespoon
   chilli flakes
½ bunch chervil, picked
2 long red chillies, thinly sliced

If you really want to impress your friends at your next dinner party or if you simply feel like spoiling yourself to a lovely lunch, then you can't go past this little number. It will take you less than 10 minutes to put together. The most important part of this recipe is to use the best-quality bread, fish and olive oil that you can. You can try it with other raw seafood if you like but I really think tuna is the best.

Preheat the oven to 170°C (325°F/Gas 3). Lay out the sliced bread on a baking tray and drizzle with the extra virgin olive oil. Place the tray in the oven and toast for 5–8 minutes until golden brown, then set aside to cool completely. Alternatively, if you prefer, you can cook the bread on a barbecue chargrill.

   Combine the diced tuna with the lemon oil and chilli oil or chilli flakes in a small bowl and stir well until the tuna is evenly coated. Season with salt and freshly ground black pepper. Gently mix in the chervil and the sliced chilli, then place a spoonful of tuna mixture evenly on each of the toasted crostini pieces and serve.

MANU'S SMOKED RAINBOW TROUT SALAD

4 SERVES

400 g (14 oz/2 whole) hot-smoked
  rainbow trout
300 g (10½ oz) kipfler (fingerling)
  potatoes, washed
1 bunch of watercress
200 g (7 oz) crème fraîche or sour cream
1 tablespoon dijon mustard
12 chives, snipped
1 granny smith apple, cored and
  thinly sliced
juice of 1 lemon
30 ml (1 fl oz) extra virgin olive oil
extra 1 tablespoon extra virgin olive oil

**One of my best mates is Manu Feildel—I had the great honour
of having him work as my head chef about 10 years ago and
since then I have worked alongside him as a judge on the
television show, *My Kitchen Rules*. I love Manu's simplicity and
restraint when it comes to putting a dish together. He taught
me this wonderful recipe, which I love because it takes hardly
any time at all to make (well once you have cooked the spuds,
that is) and it really highlights the flavour of the smoked trout.**

Take the trout fillets off the bone, remove the skin and pick out the
remaining bones left on the flesh; flake the flesh and set aside.

Cook the potatoes in boiling salted water until tender. Refresh, peel
and slice into 1 cm (½ inch) thick pieces. Pick the watercress leaves
and set aside in iced water.

Combine the crème fraîche and mustard in a bowl, then season
with salt and freshly ground black pepper. Gently stir in the potato.

To serve, place the flaked trout in a bowl. Add the watercress, chives,
apple, lemon juice and olive oil. Season with salt and freshly ground
black pepper. Arrange the potato salad on four plates, then top with
the trout mixture. Drizzle with the extra oil.

6–8 SERVES

CAJUN SPICE MIX

500 ml (17 fl oz/2 cups) sunflower oil
1 large onion, thinly sliced
10 garlic cloves, thinly sliced
1 tablespoon cayenne pepper
1 tablespoon smoked paprika
1 tablespoon celery salt
1 tablespoon dried thyme
1 teaspoon fennel seeds

2 tablespoons sunflower oil
200 g (7 oz) spicy chorizo sausage, thickly
   sliced
6–8 chicken drumsticks, skin removed
250 g (9 oz) raw prawns (shrimp), peeled
   and deveined, tails left intact, heads and
   shells reserved
1 large onion, diced
1 green capsicum (pepper), diced
1 celery stalk, diced
250 g (9 oz/1 cup) tinned diced tomatoes
3 garlic cloves, chopped
6 sprigs of thyme
2 fresh bay leaves
250 g (9 oz/1¼ cups) long-grain white rice
750 ml (26 fl oz/3 cups) chicken stock (see
   page 133)
1 tablespoon Cajun spice mix (see above)
3–4 blue swimmer crabs, cooked, halved
   and cleaned
18–24 mussels, scrubbed and beards
   removed
thinly sliced spring onions (scallions),
   to serve
chopped long green chilli, to serve
lime wedges, to serve

JAMBALAYA

Ben O'Donoghue is one chef I have a lot of respect for. Ben is a man's man, and his food is big, bold and ballsy. He has opened up his first Australian restaurant in Brisbane, called South Bank Surf Club; it is in a great location and his menu reflects the gorgeous Queensland weather. When I ate there he decided to cook his Thursday night special, jambalaya. What an amazing dish! Once I got through it I said, 'Mate, this needs to be on the menu every night,' to which he said, 'Nah, I just want to do this on Thursdays; you should see what I do on Fridays!' Funny bloke and a damn good cook.

To make the spice mix, heat the oil in a wok until hot enough to turn a small piece of bread golden brown in around 10 seconds. Cook the onion and garlic separately, moving them around constantly so they cook evenly. Remove them from the heat when they start to turn a light golden colour, and place them on paper towel to cool and drain. Place the drained and cool dried onion and garlic in a bowl, along with the remaining ingredients, and blitz with a stick blender. Any leftover spice will keep for 1 month if stored in an airtight container.

To make the jambalaya, heat the oil in a large flameproof casserole dish and cook the chorizo and chicken over medium-high heat until the chicken is golden and the chorizo is crisp. Remove with a slotted spoon, leaving the oil in the dish.

Reduce the heat to low-medium. Cook the prawn heads and shells for 5 minutes, squashing them with a potato masher to extract their flavour. Remove with a slotted spoon and discard. Add the onion, capsicum and celery and sauté until soft. Stir in the tomatoes, garlic, thyme and bay leaves and cook for 5 minutes.

Add the rice, stock, chicken and chorizo to the dish, then season with the Cajun spice mix, salt and freshly ground black pepper. Bring to a simmer, cover and cook over medium heat for 10 minutes.

Fold the crab halves into the rice, then push in the mussels and prawns. Cover and cook for a further 5 minutes. Turn off the heat and allow to rest for a few minutes.

Stir the rice to loosen it and serve the dish sprinkled with the spring onions and chopped chilli. Serve with lime wedges.

HARISSA-CRUMBED FISH WITH TABOULEH AND TAHINI SAUCE

4 SERVES

TAHINI SAUCE

2 tablespoons tahini paste

1 tablespoon extra virgin olive oil

1 garlic clove, finely minced

1 tablespoon cold water

juice of 1 lemon

TABOULEH

2 tablespoons burghul (bulgur)

1 tablespoon olive oil

400 g (14 oz) heirloom tomatoes,
    finely diced

3 tablespoons coarsely chopped mint

3 tablespoons coarsely chopped flat-leaf
    (Italian) parsley

60 g (2¼ oz/½ cup) slivered almonds,
    toasted

1 tablespoon finely chopped preserved
    lemon skin

50 g (1¾ oz/⅓ cup) pomegranate seeds

extra 3 tablespoons olive oil

juice of 1½ lemons

1 tablespoon pomegranate molasses

HARISSA CRUST

2 tablespoons harissa paste

90 g (3¼ oz/1½ cups) panko breadcrumbs

4 x 200 g (7 oz) middle-cut coral trout
    fillets, skin-on, free of all bones

pomegranate molasses, to serve

micro herbs or flat-leaf (Italian) parsley
    sprigs, to serve

Once in a while a dish comes along that really excites me; it has what I call the 'complete package' and for me that package has to contain the following: texture, flavour, aroma, eye appeal, adventurousness, playfulness, originality and, most importantly ... it must be healthy! Two boys named Clint Yudelman and Noah Rose taught me this dish and it has become one of my favourite meals to prepare at home. You can do it with just about any type of white-fleshed fish, and I have found that it works wonderfully with butterflied prawns (shrimp), too.

Preheat the oven to 180°C (350°F/Gas 4). To make the tahini sauce, whisk all the ingredients together in a small bowl.

To make the tabouleh, place the burghul in a bowl and pour in enough cold water to just cover it. Stand, covered with plastic wrap, until the water is absorbed. Using a fork, fluff it up with 1 tablespoon of olive oil and sea salt to taste. Add the tomato, herbs, almonds, preserved lemon and pomegranate seeds and mix well.

Combine the extra olive oil, lemon juice and pomegranate molasses and season with salt and freshly ground black pepper. Mix well until it forms a dressing. Add the dressing to the tabouleh and stir until it is lightly coated.

Combine all the ingredients for the harissa crust in a bowl.

Season the fish fillets with sea salt and freshly ground black pepper, then brush with a little oil. Place the fish, skin side down, in a non-stick frying pan over medium–high heat and cook for 2–3 minutes or until golden (it may be necessary to hold the fish down with a spatula so it does not curl up while cooking). Remove from the pan and place on a baking tray. Press the harissa crumb mix onto the skin side and bake for 6–8 minutes.

Serve the fish with the tahini sauce, tabouleh and a drizzling of pomegranate molasses. Garnish with micro herbs or a parsley sprig.

Note: This recipe also works well with red emperor, barramundi, kingfish, snapper or blue-eye trevalla fillets.

AIMEE'S LAKSA

4 SERVES

250 g (9 oz) rice noodles of your choosing
6 garlic cloves
200 g (7 oz) long red chillies, roughly
  chopped
2 lemongrass stems, white part only, thinly
  sliced
1 teaspoon ground turmeric
5 kaffir lime leaves, finely shredded
3 x 440 ml (15¼ fl oz) tins coconut milk
2 tablespoons grated palm sugar (jaggery)
½ teaspoon tamarind concentrate
500 g (1 lb 2 oz) barramundi fillet or other
  firm white fish fillet
50 ml (1½ fl oz) fish sauce
50 ml (1½ fl oz) lime juice
¼ Chinese cabbage (wong bok), finely
  shredded
300 g (10½ oz) firm tofu, diced into 2 cm
  (¾ inch) cubes

TO SERVE

1 handful of bean sprouts, trimmed
½ bunch of Thai basil, leaves only
crisp-fried shallots
lime halves

If you have read my other books you'll know that I have a bit of a thing for the Northern Territory. The fishing, the weather, the markets, the magnificent landscapes, the whole laid-back nature of the place—it's like there's Valium in the water up there. Each year I visit to go fishing for a few days. While there recently, my mate Steve Travia cooked me this laksa—well really he only added the seafood to it as the laksa base had already been made by his good friend, Aimee, who has a small Asian restaurant in Darwin called Warung Bu Amye. She makes paste, sauce and gives him a bucket of it to put his catch into. You can do the same thing whenever you make the paste—just make extra, freeze it, then take it away on your next fishing adventure.

Soak the noodles in a bowl of cold water for 30 minutes to soften.

Meanwhile, process the garlic, chilli, lemongrass, turmeric and lime leaves in a food processor or pound using a mortar and pestle.

Bring the coconut milk to the boil in a large heavy-based saucepan. When it starts to boil, add the blended spice paste, palm sugar and tamarind and stir well. Add the barramundi, bring back to the boil, then turn off the heat and let it sit for 5 minutes, or until the fish is just cooked through. Break the fish into large pieces.

Add the fish sauce, lime juice, cabbage and tofu. Turn the heat back on and cook for a further minute, then remove from the heat.

Divide the noodles and fish among four bowls, spoon over the laksa and garnish with the bean sprouts, basil leaves and crisp-fried shallots. Serve with lime halves.

KANGAROO ISLAND WHITING BURGER

4 SERVES

vegetable oil, for deep-frying
4 x 140 g (5 oz) King George whiting fillets
4 long sesame seed bread rolls
softened butter
½ iceberg lettuce, finely shredded
2 tomatoes, sliced
1 Lebanese (short) cucumber, sliced
2 tablespoons mayonnaise
1 small handful of flat-leaf (Italian)
    parsley, chopped
lemon wedges, to serve

TEMPURA BATTER

185 ml (6 fl oz/¾ cup) cold soda water
    (club soda)
1 free-range egg, lightly beaten
60 g (2¼ oz/½ cup) cornflour (cornstarch)
60 g (2¼ oz) plain (all-purpose) flour

On my first trip to Kangaroo Island in South Australia, I drove from one side of the island to the other to do some dune surfing on the huge sand dunes. I was starving so I pulled into Vivonne Bay and went to the general store. As soon as I read on their blackboard the words 'world famous whiting burger', I was sold. A few minutes later out came the most delicious fish burger I have ever tried—King George whiting, battered and fried, served with tomato, shredded iceberg lettuce, sliced cucumber, chopped parsley and mayonnaise on a sesame seed wholemeal roll. Yum! Here is my recreation of that burger.

To make the batter, whisk the soda water and egg together. Combine the cornflour and plain flour in a bowl and slowly whisk in the egg-soda water mixture with a chopstick or wooden spoon until the batter is the consistency of pouring cream. Do not overmix.

Pour oil to a depth of 1 cm (½ inch) into a 22 cm (8½ inch) saucepan over medium heat. Test the oil by dropping a little batter into the pan; it will sizzle when the oil is hot. Dip a fish fillet into the batter and coat well. Pick up the fillet with a fork and drain the excess batter into the bowl, then carefully lay the fish in the pan. Repeat, cooking a couple at a time for 2–3 minutes each side until lightly golden. Drain on paper towel.

Cut the bread rolls in half and lightly butter them. Lay the lettuce on the base, then top with tomato, cucumber and battered fish. Add a little mayonnaise and sprinkle with chopped parsley. Serve with lemon wedges and shoestring fries.

MUSSELS WITH CHILLI BEAN PASTE AND CHOY SUM

4 SERVES

80 ml (2½ fl oz/⅓ cup) vegetable oil
80 ml (2½ fl oz/⅓ cup) Chinese chilli
  bean paste
1 tablespoon finely chopped fresh ginger
1 tablespoon minced garlic
330 ml (11¼ fl oz/1⅓ cups) fish stock
2 kg (4 lb 8 oz) black mussels, scrubbed
  and beards removed
100 ml (3½ fl oz) Chinese rice wine
½ teaspoon black Chinese vinegar
1 teaspoon white sugar
2 teaspoons light soy sauce
1¼ teaspoons cornflour (cornstarch) mixed
  with 1 teaspoon cold water
3 spring onions (scallions), green part only,
  sliced
2 bunches choy sum, cut into 2.5 cm
  (1 inch) pieces
½ bunch of coriander (cilantro), leaves
  only (optional)

I love when you create a new dish that is an immediate hit, which is what happened with this recipe. I was having a beer with my good mate John Susman and he gave me a kilo of new season small mussels from Port Lincoln in South Australia (which in my opinion is where the best mussels in Australia come from). When I got home all I had was a bunch of choy sum in the fridge and some aromatics. So out came the wok and in went a bit of this and a bit of that ... the result was so good that we now cook this at least once a month. Mussels are one of the best sources of omega-3 you can get and they are so cheap that I think everyone should eat them at least once a fortnight.

Heat the oil in a wok over medium heat. When it is hot, add the chilli bean paste and stir-fry for 2 minutes until fragrant. Add the ginger and garlic and stir-fry for another 2 minutes until the garlic turns lightly golden. Pour in the stock, turn up the heat and bring to the boil. Season with salt and freshly ground black pepper. Remove from the heat.

Discard any broken mussels, or open ones that don't close when tapped on the workbench. Preheat a large saucepan over high heat. Add the wine and mussels, cover with a lid and steam until the mussels open, discarding any mussels that don't open.

Drain the liquid from the pan, reserving 100 ml (3½ fl oz) of it. Return the reserved cooking liquid to the pan and add the chilli bean sauce, vinegar, sugar, soy sauce and the cornflour mixture. Stir in the mussels and bring back to the boil. Toss in the spring onion and choy sum and cook for 1 minute until the choy sum is tender. Sprinkle with coriander leaves, if you like.

PANKO-CRUMBED FISH WITH ARTICHOKE TARTARE

4 SERVES

ARTICHOKE TARTARE

2 free-range egg yolks
2 garlic cloves, chopped
4 small artichoke hearts from a jar
juice of 1 lemon
10 mint leaves, chopped
2 tablespoons salted capers, rinsed
  and drained
2 teaspoons fish sauce
50 ml (1½ fl oz) peanut oil
50 ml (1½ fl oz) vegetable oil

75 g (2½ oz/½ cup) plain (all-purpose) flour
2 free-range eggs, lightly beaten
90 g (3¼ oz/1½ cups) panko breadcrumbs
700 g (1 lb 9 oz) flathead fillets or other
  white-fleshed fish, skin and bones
  removed
185 ml (6 fl oz/¾ cup) grapeseed oil
lemon wedges, to serve

This meal was served to me by my good mate, Nick Hannaford, who lives on Kangaroo Island in South Australia. Nick loves to entertain and show you the beauty of his home town, whether it be admiring the natural magnificence of the coastline while fishing from his boat or exploring the local food producers on the island. Nick is quite a natural in the kitchen and it shows with this simple dish.

To make the tartare, place the egg yolks, garlic, artichoke hearts, lemon juice, mint, capers and fish sauce in a food processor, and blend. Slowly add the oils and keep mixing until it forms a thick consistency, then season with salt and freshly ground black pepper.

Place the flour in a shallow bowl, the egg in another and the panko crumbs in a third. Lightly season the fish with some sea salt, then lightly dust with the flour, coat in the egg then, lastly, firmly press on the panko crumbs.

Heat the oil in a frying pan over medium-high heat and fry the fish for 30–45 seconds until golden and crispy, then turn over and cook for a further 30 seconds until crispy on that side.

Drain on kitchen paper to remove the excess oil. Serve with lemon wedges and artichoke tartare.

PAD THAI
WITH PRAWNS

4 SERVES

375 g (13 oz) dried thin rice noodles
2 tablespoons dried shrimp
2 tablespoon white sugar
2 tablespoons tamarind concentrate
2 tablespoons oyster sauce
80 ml (2½ fl oz/⅓ cup) fish sauce
2 tablespoons water
50 ml (1½ fl oz) peanut oil
4 red Asian shallots, sliced
2 free-range eggs
100 g (3½ oz) firm tofu, chopped into 1 cm
    (½ inch) cubes
½ teaspoon chilli powder
200 g (7 oz) bean sprouts, trimmed
1 bunch garlic chives, chop three-quarters
    of the bunch into 1 cm (½ inch) batons
    and the remainder into 6 cm (2½ inch)
    batons for garnish (optional)
2 tablespoons toasted peanuts, finely
    chopped
1 lime, cut into wedges
extra 1 tablespoon chilli powder

The very first Thai dish I ever ate was Pad Thai; it wasn't in Thailand but at a cheap Thai takeaway joint in Melbourne when I was an apprentice chef. I fell in love straight away and decided that I needed to learn to make Pad Thai myself so I could cook it for my mates and myself whenever I wanted to. This is the resulting dish that I've cooked hundreds of times at home since then—I hope you like it as much as I do.

Soak the noodles in cold water for 1 hour until they are soft. Drain.

Soak the dried shrimp in water for 10 minutes or until just soft.

Put the sugar, tamarind, oyster sauce, fish sauce and water in a small saucepan and heat over low heat until the sugar dissolves.

Heat 1½ tablespoons of the peanut oil in a large wok over medium heat and cook the shallots until just starting to colour. Crack the eggs into the wok and reduce the heat to prevent the eggs from burning. Mix in the tofu, soaked shrimp and the noodles. Turn the heat up, add the remaining oil and stir-fry for 1-2 minutes, allowing the noodles to colour a little. Add the tamarind sauce mixture to the wok and mix well, then simmer for 1-2 minutes.

Add the chilli powder, half the bean sprouts and the short garlic chive batons, and cook for another 30 seconds. Check the seasoning.

Pile the noodles on a plate and top with the remaining bean sprouts and long garlic chive batons, if you like. Serve with the peanuts, lime wedges and chilli powder on the side.

PRAWN WON TON SOUP

4 SERVES

FILLING

300 g (10½ oz) raw prawn (shrimp) meat, finely minced

1 tablespoon finely grated fresh ginger

4 dried or fresh shiitake mushrooms (if dried, soak in warm water until soft), finely chopped

4 water chestnuts, finely chopped

2 spring onions (scallions), white part only, finely chopped

1 free-range egg white

28 won ton wrappers

1 teaspoon cornflour (cornstarch), mixed with 1 tablespoon of water

2 litres (8 cups) chicken stock (see page 133)

5 cm (2 inch) knob of fresh ginger, peeled and thinly sliced

1 lemongrass stem, white part only, bruised and cut in half

1 tablespoon light soy sauce

400 g (14 oz) choy sum, cut into 3 cm (1¼ inch) lengths

2 spring onions (scallions), green part only, sliced

2 long red chillies, seeds removed and thinly sliced

I often sit in Chinese restaurants and admire the deftness and agility of the chefs as they assemble won tons. It's not hard to make won tons at home and even though you probably won't make them with the same degree of grace, precision and speed as a dumpling master, the flavour will be just as good.

To make the filling, combine the prawn meat, ginger, mushroom, water chestnuts, spring onions, egg white and salt and freshly ground black pepper in a bowl and mix well until all the ingredients are well combined. Refrigerate for 1 hour.

Lay the won ton wrappers on a workbench. Working with one wrapper at a time, put 1 teaspoon of the filling in the centre of the wrapper. Dip your finger in the cornflour paste and run it around the edge of the wrapper. Fold over to form a triangle, pressing the edges together. Bring the two corners together to meet and overlap in the middle, then seal with a little more of the cornflour paste. Set aside, then repeat with the remaining wrappers and filling.

Heat the stock in a saucepan over medium heat, add the ginger, lemongrass and soy sauce and bring to a simmer.

Blanch the choy sum in boiling water for 1 minute, then drain and add to the stock. Place the won tons in the stock, return to the boil and cook for 2 minutes or until the won tons rise to the top. Discard the ginger and lemongrass and ladle the soup into serving bowls with seven won tons per bowl. Garnish with spring onion and chilli.

PERUVIAN CEVICHE OF CORAL TROUT

4 SERVES

600 g (1 lb 5 oz) coral trout fillet, cleaned,
    skin removed and pin boned (see Note)
1 teaspoon chopped fresh ginger
2 tablespoons chopped celery
1 garlic clove
½ bunch coriander (cilantro), leaves picked,
    reserve the stalks
2 long red chillies, sliced
juice of 6 limes
1 red onion, thinly sliced
90 ml (3 fl oz) chilled vodka
extra long red chilli, seeds removed and
    sliced, for garnish
extra coriander (cilantro) leaves,
    for garnish

I do a lot of entertaining at home and also with my job as a
high-end caterer, and one thing I have learned is that you have
to have fun when entertaining both at home and professionally.
That is where a dish like this comes into play. It is super simple
to prepare and a lot of fun to make with your guests—just be
careful if someone is driving home to make sure they miss out
on the shot of vodka. 'What is the shot of vodka for?' you may
ask. Well, let's just say it definitely livens up the party! Make
sure you only ever attempt a raw seafood dish when you have
the freshest seafood. There can be no excuses: if it is raw, it must
be straight out of the ocean or from a trusted supplier.

Dice the coral trout fillet into 2 cm (¾ inch) cubes and place in a
chilled bowl.
   Purée the ginger, celery, garlic, coriander stalks and 1 of the sliced
red chillies in a small food processor. Add the lime juice to the purée
and mix. Add the purée to the fish. Add the rest of the sliced red
chilli, coriander leaves and the onion and mix with the vodka. Leave
to sit for 25 minutes. Season with salt.
   Serve on a small platter and add extra chilli and picked coriander
for garnish.

Note: You can make this with any very fresh white-fleshed fish,
scallops or prawns (shrimp).

BLUE SWIMMER CRAB LINGUINE

4 SERVES

80 g (2¾ oz) butter
8 garlic cloves, sliced
2 bird's eye chillies, diced
6 French shallots, sliced
2 tablespoons chopped coriander (cilantro) root and stem
100 ml (3½ fl oz) fish sauce
1 litre (35 fl oz/4 cups) vegetable stock, fish stock or water
24 cherry tomatoes, halved
500 g (1 lb 2 oz) linguine
320 g (11¼ oz) cooked blue swimmer crabmeat (or use other crabmeat)
1 bunch of coriander (cilantro), leaves only, chopped
extra 4 sprigs of coriander (cilantro)
lime wedges (optional)

This is the dish that really helped to put my restaurants on the map and one I've cooked at least 50,000 times (I reckon I have nailed it now ... ha-ha). It's got a lot going for it—it is easy, impressive and moreish. It has a fair amount of butter so treat it as an occasional dish, perfect for a celebration. Make sure you buy the best possible crabmeat for this or simply substitute prawns (shrimp). If you prefer, you can make it with noodles instead of linguine, as it does have some Asian flavours.

Heat the butter in a frying pan, then sauté the garlic, chilli, shallot, and coriander root and stem until golden. Add the fish sauce and cook for about 10 seconds to release the flavour. Add the stock and tomatoes and reduce until you have a sauce that is thick enough to coat the pasta.

Meanwhile, cook the linguine in a large saucepan of boiling salted water until al dente. Drain.

Toss the pasta with the sauce and add the cooked crabmeat and chopped coriander leaves. Serve in bowls and garnish with coriander sprigs and a squeeze of lime, if you like.

Note: Don't add any salt to the sauce as the fish sauce is salty enough.

SALMON WITH PEA PURÉE AND RED RADISH SALAD

4 SERVES

4 x 160–180 g (5½–6 oz) salmon fillets,
  skin on, pin boned
2 tablespoons olive oil
20 g (¾ oz) fresh horseradish, peeled and
  grated, for garnish

PEA PURÉE
650 g (1 lb 7 oz/5 cups) frozen peas, thawed
1 tablespoon water

HONEY MUSTARD SAUCE
2 tablespoons dijon mustard
2 tablespoons organic honey
1 free-range egg yolk
juice of 2 lemons
80 ml (2½ fl oz/⅓ cup) olive oil

RED RADISH SALAD
1 small handful of podded broad (fava)
  beans (if using frozen, thaw and remove
  the skins)
¼ bunch of red radishes, thinly sliced
¼ fennel bulb, thinly sliced
⅓ cup chervil, picked or micro parsley or
  watercress
3 tablespoons thinly sliced celery hearts
  (yellow centre ribs of the celery), leaves
  picked and stalks thinly sliced
juice of 1 lemon
2 tablespoons extra virgin olive oil

This dish is based on one that has been on my menu at Hugos Manly for years now. My executive chef, Massimo Mele, created it and I won't let him take it off the menu (sorry Massimo but the customers love it and so do I). There is the lusciousness of the rich omega-3 laden salmon fillet, the subtleness of the pea purée and the heat from the freshly grated horseradish all with a simple radish salad to enliven the palate between each bite. The best thing about this dish is that you can have it on the table in about 20 minutes. You could substitute ocean trout, rainbow trout or kingfish for the salmon, if you prefer.

To make the honey mustard sauce, place the mustard, honey, egg yolk and lemon juice in a bowl, season with salt and freshly ground black pepper and whisk well. While still whisking, slowly add the oil until the mixture is pale in colour and is a pouring consistency.

To make the pea purée, place the thawed peas in a blender and add the water. Blend the peas until smooth, then season with salt and freshly ground black pepper to taste. Pass through a sieve to allow the purée to become a smooth consistency, then set to one side—we normally serve the pea purée at room temperature.

Lightly coat the fish with 1 tablespoon of oil and season with salt and freshly ground black pepper. Heat the remaining oil in a frying pan over medium-high heat and cook the fish, skin side down, for 1-2 minutes, or until the skin is golden, then flip the fish over and cook for a further 2 minutes, or until the fish is medium-rare.

Meanwhile, to make the salad, blanch the broad beans in boiling, salted water, then drain and place in iced water to cool down enough to remove the skins. Combine the peeled broad beans with the radish, fennel, chervil and celery heart in a bowl. Add the lemon juice and extra virgin olive oil, season with salt and freshly ground black pepper and toss well.

Spread 2 tablespoons of the pea purée onto each serving plate and add a little of the mustard sauce. Place the fish on top and serve with the red radish salad and fresh horseradish.

NIHIWATU SEAFOOD CURRY

6 SERVES

CURRY PASTE

4 red Asian shallots, roughly chopped
6 garlic cloves, roughly chopped
1 bird's eye chilli, roughly chopped
3 candlenuts, roughly chopped
2 cm (¾ inch) knob of fresh turmeric,
  peeled and chopped or 1 teaspoon
  ground turmeric
1.5 cm (⅝ inch) knob of fresh galangal,
  peeled and chopped
2 lemongrass stems, white part only,
  chopped
1 cm (½ inch) knob of fresh ginger, peeled
  and chopped
1 tablespoon coriander seeds
1 tablespoon vegetable oil

3 tablespoons vegetable oil
600 g (1 lb 5 oz) raw king prawns (shrimp),
  peeled and deveined, tails left intact
500 g (1 lb 2 oz) squid tubes, cleaned and
  cut into cubes
500 g (1 lb 2 oz) fish fillet, cut into cubes
4 lemongrass stems, smashed
3 long red chillies, seeds removed and
  sliced
4 kaffir lime leaves
6 tablespoons curry paste (see method)
500 ml (17 fl oz/2 cups) coconut milk
pinch of sugar
coriander (cilantro) leaves, for garnish
lime wedges, to serve (optional)

One of the best aspects of my job is that I get to travel to wonderful locations and teach people to cook. On a recent trip to the Indonesian island of Sumba, I was teaching at what must be the most beautiful resort in the world, Nihiwatu. Not only is it breathtaking, more importantly the resort takes an ethical approach to tourism and helps the Sumbanese people with health care, clean water and education. I was treated to wonderful hospitality from the owner, Claude Graves, and his staff, in particular the executive chef of the resort, Andi Cahyono. Andi showed me his seafood curry that uses freshly caught seafood, and I am honoured that he has allowed me to share his recipe with you. For more information on preventing poverty in Sumba, go to www.sumbafoundation.org.

To make the curry paste, blend all the ingredients, except the oil, together in a food processor. Heat the oil in a saucepan and sauté the curry paste until fragrant.

Heat the oil in a wok or large saucepan over medium heat, add the mixed seafood, lemongrass, chilli, lime leaves and curry paste. Pour in the coconut milk and bring to the boil. Simmer until the seafood is just cooked. Season with salt, freshly ground black pepper and a little sugar. Garnish with coriander leaves and serve with lime wedges and rice.

GARLIC AND CHILLI PRAWNS WITH BLOOD ORANGE AND FENNEL SALAD

4 SERVES

100 g (3½ oz) fennel, about 1 bulb

4 large blood oranges

125 ml (4 fl oz/½ cup) extra virgin olive oil

3 tablespoons white wine vinegar

⅓ cup finely chopped flat-leaf (Italian) parsley

800 g (1 lb 12 oz) cooked tiger prawns (shrimp) or other prawns, peeled and deveined, tails left intact

1 long red chilli, seeds removed and finely chopped

2 garlic cloves, minced

This is a slight variation on a recipe by my good mates Shadi and Veronica Abraham. This is my type of food—three great ingredients with very little done to them to create what could be one of the nicest summer lunches or starters ever. The key to this dish is to source only the freshest ingredients available: if you can't get beautiful ripe citrus fruit or the freshest fennel and prawns, then cook something else. Blood oranges have a very short season but you can substitute other varieties of orange or grapefruit for them and you will still have an outstanding dish.

To make the salad, wash the fennel and discard the outer bulb—you need to use the inner part/heart of the fennel bulb. Thinly slice or shave the fennel and place in a bowl.

Peel the oranges and remove as much of the white pith as you can. Remove the seeds. Slice the oranges in rounds about 5 mm (¼ inch) thick. Add to the bowl with the fennel.

To make the dressing, mix half the oil with 1 teaspoon of the vinegar and pour over the oranges and fennel. Season to taste with salt and freshly ground black pepper and sprinkle half the parsley through the salad to give it some colour. Toss to combine and allow to marinate for at least 10 minutes.

Place the prawns in a bowl and add the chilli, garlic and the remaining oil, vinegar and parsley. Season to taste. Toss to combine. Allow to marinate for 15 minutes before serving. Layer the salad onto plates, then arrange the prawns on top.

NONNA'S BOILED OCTOPUS WITH POTATO, GARLIC, CHILLI AND OLIVE OIL

6 SERVES

1 kg (2 lb 4 oz) octopus tentacles
3 large kipfler (fingerling) potatoes
5 garlic cloves, lightly smashed
1 long red chilli, sliced (seeds removed,
    if you prefer mild hotness)
1 tablespoon chopped flat-leaf (Italian)
    parsley
1 tablespoon chopped marjoram
250 ml (9 fl oz/1 cup) white wine vinegar
250 ml (9 fl oz/1 cup) mild extra virgin
    olive oil
extra white wine vinegar, to serve

This recipe is from Massimo Mele, the executive chef at Hugos; his nonna used to cook this for him during summertime when he was a little kid on the Amalfi Coast. It's easy to make and absolutely delicious.

Place a large saucepan of sea water over high heat and bring to the boil. If sea water is unattainable, add 730 g (1 lb 10 oz/2 cups) of rock salt to 5 litres (20 cups) of water and bring to the boil.

Blanch the octopus three times in boiling water for about 5 seconds each time. Once complete, turn the heat down and add the octopus and potatoes to the same pan. Gently simmer for about 45 minutes, or until tender. Remove the octopus from the pan and set aside. If the potatoes need longer, cook them until they are tender. Let the potatoes cool down in the salty water.

Once the octopus is cool enough to handle, chop it into 5 cm (2 inch) pieces and put in a non-reactive bowl.

Peel and slice the potato into discs, add to the bowl with the octopus, then add all the remaining ingredients. Leave to marinate for 48 hours in the refrigerator.

Remove the garlic. Season with more vinegar and season with freshly ground black pepper. It shouldn't need any salt.

POULTRY

CHICKEN BIRYANI

8 SERVES

ROGAN JOSH CURRY POWDER

2½ teaspoons ground coriander seeds
2 teaspoons ground cumin
1 teaspoon mild paprika
½ teaspoon chilli powder
½ teaspoon ground ginger
½ teaspoon ground turmeric
¼ teaspoon ground fennel seeds
¼ teaspoon freshly grated nutmeg
¼ teaspoon ground cardamom seeds
¼ teaspoon ground cloves

CHAI MASALA

3 cm (1¼ inch) cinnamon stick, crushed
6 whole cloves
4 cardamom pods

One country I'm dying to visit is India. I've been reading a lot of Indian-based novels over the past few years and I'm always swept into the world of colourful characters, the rich and poor living side by side in a chaotic way of life, but the thing that seems to bind them all and is at the very heart of their existence is their love of their cuisine. I cook Indian food quite a lot at home, from simple dhals, to naan bread with garlic and lovely aromatic korma dishes, but when I want something that is a little bit special, I always cook this wonderful chicken biryani. I love the texture and full-bodied flavour of this dish—the dried fruit, almonds, onions, yoghurt-cooked chicken and, of course, the rice. This is as close to India that I can get at the moment ... but it isn't a bad place to start.

To make the rogan josh curry powder, put all the spices in a spice grinder and blend until you have a fine powder.

To make the chai masala, put all the spices in a spice grinder and blend until you have a fine powder.

MARINADE

1 tablespoon plain yoghurt
1 tablespoon chai masala (see opposite)
2 tablespoons rogan josh curry powder
(see opposite)
1 teaspoon minced garlic
1 teaspoon grated fresh ginger
1 teaspoon sea salt
1 tablespoon vegetable oil

1 kg (2 lb 4 oz) organic or good-quality
chicken thighs

RICE

12 saffron threads
2 tablespoons warm milk
400 g (14 oz/2 cups) basmati rice, rinsed
and drained
1 tablespoon currants
2 tablespoons slivered almonds, toasted
2 tablespoons vegetable oil
1 large onion, sliced

TO SERVE

coriander (cilantro) leaves
mint leaves
plain yoghurt
lemon halves

To make the marinade, put the yoghurt, chai masala, curry powder, garlic, ginger, salt and oil in a non-reactive dish and mix together. Add the chicken thighs, coat in the mixture, then marinate in the refrigerator for 2 hours or overnight if time permits.

Preheat the oven to 180°C (350°F/Gas 4). In a small bowl soak the saffron in the warm milk and set aside.

Parboil the rice in 500 ml (17 fl oz/2 cups) of boiling water for 6 minutes, drain, then mix the currants and almonds through the rice and set to one side.

Meanwhile, heat half the oil in a large saucepan over medium-high heat. Add the marinated chicken to the pan and seal the chicken until golden. Remove from the heat. At the same time, heat the other tablespoon of oil in a frying pan and sauté the onion until golden.

Spoon half of the rice mixture into a 3 litre (12 cup), 28 x 20 x 8 cm (11¼ x 8 x 3¼ inch) casserole dish and place the chicken pieces on top. Deglaze the chicken pan with 60 ml (2 fl oz/¼ cup) of water and pour over the chicken. Spread the cooked onions over the chicken, then cover with the remaining rice, pressing down gently with the back of the spoon. Drizzle the saffron and milk over the rice. Cover tightly with foil or a lid and bake for 40 minutes. Serve with coriander, mint, yoghurt and lemon halves.

WHITE-CUT CHICKEN (HAINANESE CHICKEN) WITH SPRING ONION DRESSING

6 SERVES

DRESSING

80 ml (2½ fl oz/⅓ cup) peanut oil
4 dried red chillies
2 spring onions (scallions), finely sliced,
    reserving the green for the garnish
1 large knob of fresh ginger, finely diced
2 garlic cloves, finely chopped
3 tablespoons Chinese rice wine
100 ml (3½ fl oz) rice vinegar
1 tablespoon salt
1 tablespoon caster (superfine) sugar

1 x 1.6 kg (3 lb 8 oz) organic or good-
    quality chicken
3 litres (12 cups) water

RELISH

125 ml (4 fl oz/½ cup) white wine vinegar
115 g (4 oz/½ cup) caster (superfine) sugar
170 ml (5½ fl oz/⅔ cup) water
2 Lebanese (short) cucumbers, washed,
    quartered lengthways and sliced (about
    1 cup)
8 red Asian shallots
⅓ cup julienned fresh ginger
1 long red chilli, thinly sliced

I still remember the first time I ate this dish—it was the beautiful texture of the chicken that has stayed with me. The chicken is poached whole, then steeped so the flesh becomes soft and silky. You can serve it with various dipping sauces. Here I have matched it with the traditional ginger and spring onion dressing to keep it Chinese but it works just as well with a South-east Asian dressing and a crunchy green salad.

To make the dressing, heat the oil in a wok over medium heat and cook the chillies until blackened. Discard the chillies and leave the oil to cool. In a bowl, combine the spring onion, ginger, garlic, rice wine, vinegar, salt and sugar, then add to the cooled oil. Leave to stand for 1 hour to allow the flavours to infuse into the oil.

Meanwhile, remove the fat from the cavity of the chicken, rinse the chicken in cold water and pat dry with paper towel. In a saucepan large enough to fit the chicken, bring the water to a boil. Place the chicken into the pan and return to the boil. Place a lid on top of the pan and simmer for 15 minutes.

Meanwhile make the relish. Combine the vinegar, sugar and water in a small saucepan and bring to the boil. Remove from the heat when the sugar has dissolved. Set aside to cool. Mix the remaining ingredients in a bowl and pour the syrup over the top.

Remove the pan with the chicken from the heat and leave the chicken to steep for 20 minutes. During this time do not remove the lid or the heat will be lost and the chicken will not cook. After 20 minutes, remove the lid and carefully lift the chicken from the stock. Drain on paper towel and chop Chinese-style through the bone, then put on a platter.

Pour the spring onion dressing over the chicken, garnish with the green spring onion pieces and serve with the relish and rice.

THE PANTRY'S CHICKEN CAESAR SALAD

4 SERVES

DRESSING

1 free-range egg yolk
4 anchovies, chopped
½ garlic clove
1 tablespoon lemon juice
1 teaspoon dijon mustard
250 ml (9 fl oz/1 cup) light olive oil
1 tablespoon water, if needed

8 slices of pancetta
2 tablespoons olive oil
3 thick-cut slices of good-quality bread, cut
   into 2 cm (¾ inch) cubes
4 free-range eggs, at room temperature
8 organic or good-quality chicken
   tenderloins
1 garlic clove, minced
2 baby cos (romaine) lettuces
1 large handful of flat-leaf (Italian) parsley
4 white anchovies, rinsed and halved
   (optional)
parmesan shavings, to serve (optional)

The first restaurant I opened was The Pantry in Melbourne's bayside suburb of Brighton about 20 years ago. One dish that has been on the menu since day one is the Caesar salad. The beauty of this dish is not only the creamy dressing, but the croutons, the crispy bacon, salty anchovies, the cos lettuce, parmesan cheese and the soft coddled eggs. I love to add some chicken to it to make it into a meal.

To make the dressing, combine the egg yolk, anchovies, garlic, lemon juice, mustard and salt in a food processor or blender. Process briefly until combined. With the motor running, gradually add the oil, drop by drop until the dressing has emulsified and thickened slightly. Add the oil a little faster until you have added it all and the dressing has the consistency of pouring cream. Check the seasoning, adding more salt, some freshly ground black pepper or extra lemon juice as desired. If the dressing is too thick, add the water.

Heat a little of the oil in a frying pan over medium heat and cook the pancetta until crisp and golden, then remove from the pan with tongs and drain on paper towel. Add the bread cubes to the same pan with a little extra olive oil, stirring until crisp and golden; drain the croutons on paper towel.

Meanwhile, place the eggs in a saucepan and cover with cold water, bring to the boil over high heat and cook until soft boiled (about 4 minutes). Drain and cool under running water. Peel, cut in half and set aside.

Wipe the frying pan clean and heat 1 tablespoon of the oil. Rub the chicken tenderloins with the garlic and some salt and freshly ground black pepper and pan-fry until cooked through and golden; set aside.

Wash the cos well and cut into wedges. Arrange in serving bowls with the parsley and anchovies, if using. Top with shards of pancetta, sliced chicken, egg and croutons. Season. Drizzle with dressing and, if you like, top with shaved parmesan.

AYU'S BALINESE ROASTED CHICKEN

4 SERVES

10 garlic cloves, finely chopped
6 long red chillies, finely chopped
1 knob of fresh ginger, finely chopped
1 small finger of turmeric, finely chopped
6 red Asian shallots, finely chopped
80 ml (2½ fl oz/⅓ cup) grapeseed oil
1 x 1.8 kg (4 lb) corn-fed chicken
4 limes
10 fresh bay leaves

I thought I had tried every roast chicken recipe known to man; that was until I spent a few nights in Bali recently. I was staying with local wild man Nicholas Morley, and he and his friend, Ayu, prepared this chicken dish. I couldn't believe how easy it was to make, then in a few hours I was savouring every delicious mouthful. If there is only one recipe you can try from this book, it should definitely be this one.

Combine the finely chopped garlic, chilli, ginger, turmeric and shallots in a small bowl. Heat a small frying pan with some of the oil, then fry off the aromatic garlicky paste over low heat until fragrant. Remove from the heat and set aside to cool.

When the paste has cooled, take a large sheet of foil and place the chicken in the centre. Slice the limes into quarters, then squeeze the juice over the chicken and rub the lime quarters into the skin. Wearing gloves, rub the cooled paste all over the skin of the chicken and inside the cavity. Place the lime quarters inside the chicken and season the entire chicken with salt and freshly ground black pepper. Lay the bay leaves on top of the chicken and wrap tightly in the foil. Leave to marinate in the refrigerator for a few hours or overnight if time permits.

Preheat the oven to 180°C (350°F/Gas 4). Keep the chicken wrapped in the foil, place it in a baking tray and bake for 1½–1¾ hours. Remove from the oven and allow to rest for 10 minutes before opening. Serve with rice.

JACINTA'S FRIED CHICKEN

4 SERVES

vegetable oil, for deep-frying
1 free-range egg, beaten
500 ml (17 fl oz/2 cups) buttermilk
125 g (4½ oz/1 cup) cornflour (cornstarch)
1 teaspoon chilli powder
1½ teaspoons dried oregano
1 teaspoon dried marjoram
2 teaspoons dried basil
2 teaspoons ground black pepper
2 teaspoons salt
1 teaspoon paprika
2 teaspoons ground cumin
1½ teaspoons garlic powder
1½ teaspoons onion powder
1 teaspoon chicken stock powder
2 tablespoons dry breadcrumbs
1 x 1.8 kg (4 lb) organic or good-quality
    chicken, cut into 10 pieces
sweet chilli sauce, to serve
aïoli, to serve (see page 203)

My head chef at Hugos is Jacinta Cannataci and she often makes this as a staff meal for us—I think it's everyone's favourite. Jacinta has given me the recipe and I've made it at home a number of times and it gets the same enthusiastic reaction at home as it does at staff meal times. I always serve it with a fresh salad so I have a well-rounded meal. Give it a go and I'm sure you'll love it as much as we all do.

Preheat the oil in your deep-fryer to 170°C (325°F) or fill a large heavy-based saucepan one-third full of oil and heat until it reaches the correct temperature.

Beat the egg and buttermilk in a small bowl and set to one side.

In another bowl, combine the dry ingredients and mix well.

Place the chicken pieces in the buttermilk–egg mix, turn until well coated, then place in the flour mixture and completely coat the chicken in flour.

Fry the chicken in batches for 10–12 minutes, or until cooked through. Remove from the deep-fryer and drain the excess oil on paper towel. Serve with the sweet chilli sauce and aïoli.

MUM'S CHICKEN AND CORN SOUP

4 SERVES

CHICKEN STOCK

2 kg (4 lb 8 oz) chicken bones
2 carrots, halved
1 onion, peeled and halved
2 celery stalks, halved
4 flat-leaf (Italian) parsley stalks
2 sprigs of thyme
1 bay leaf
1 teaspoon black peppercorns

1.25 litres (5 cups) chicken stock (see recipe above)
500 g (1 lb 2 oz) organic or good-quality chicken thigh fillets
2 x 400 g (14 oz) tins creamed corn
2 spring onions (scallions), sliced
1 teaspoon cornflour (cornstarch), mixed with 2 tablespoons water
2 free-range eggs, lightly beaten
salt and white pepper, to taste
100 g (3½ oz/2 cups) baby English spinach leaves
extra 1 spring onion (scallion), sliced lengthways into shreds or 2 tablespoons chopped flat-leaf (Italian) parsley

This book is about what I eat at home. Well it wouldn't really be complete without including my mum's chicken and corn soup. I must admit that I don't actually cook this dish myself, but Mum lives across the road from me and brings this to my house for the kids to eat at least once a fortnight as it is one of their favourites, just as it has been one of my favourites for the past 30 years or so. So thanks, Mum, you've looked after me all these years and now you're helping my kids appreciate good food, too. Love ya.

To make the stock, rinse the chicken bones under cold running water and place in a large saucepan. Add the rest of the stock ingredients and add enough water to cover. Bring to the boil, skimming off any scum from the surface. Reduce the heat to low and gently simmer for 2 hours. Remove from the heat, then strain and cool to room temperature. Refrigerate for 2-3 hours or until chilled and the fat has settled on the surface. Remove and discard the fat. Refrigerate and use within 3 days or freeze for up to 3 months. Makes about 4 litres (16 cups).

To make the soup, pour the chicken stock into a saucepan over medium-high heat and bring to the boil. Turn down to a simmer and add the chicken thighs. Poach the chicken for 6 minutes, or until just cooked through. Remove from the stock, finely shred and set aside.

Add the creamed corn and spring onion to the stock and bring back up to a simmer. Add the chicken, whisk in the cornflour mixture and cook for a further 1-2 minutes to make the soup a slightly thick consistency. Once the soup starts to thicken, slowly stir in the egg with a wooden spoon and season to taste with salt and white pepper. Add the spinach and stir through, then garnish with spring onion or parsley.

POLDI'S CHICKEN AND TOFU DISH

4 SERVES

2–3 tablespoons vegetable oil

350 g (12 oz) organic or good-quality
  chicken thigh fillets, diced

2 free-range egg whites

1 small knob of fresh ginger

4 garlic cloves

1 long red chilli, chopped

1¼ tablespoons sesame oil

2 tablespoons oyster sauce

2 tablespoons cornflour (cornstarch),
  mixed with 200 ml (7 fl oz) water

250 g (9 oz) packet of silken tofu, cut into
  2 cm x 1 cm (¾ x ½ inch) pieces

½ bunch of coriander (cilantro), leaves
  only, chopped

4 spring onions (scallions), thinly sliced
  lengthways

2 teaspoons sesame seeds, toasted

chilli oil (optional)

This is a recipe I have eaten countless times at my mother-in-law's house. You can substitute green vegetables for the tofu if you prefer, but I love the silky texture that the tofu imparts. I would much rather a dish taste, smell and feel good in the mouth than it look good on the plate. In so many magazines and cookbooks you see great pictures of food, but the dishes lack soul ... not this one.

Heat the oil in a frying pan and cook the chicken in two batches for 5 minutes, cooking on all sides. Remove from the pan and set aside.

Marinate the chicken pieces in the egg white for 10 minutes.

Using a mortar and pestle, pound the ginger, garlic and chilli with a pinch of salt.

Add 1 tablespoon of sesame oil to a wok and heat over medium heat. Add the gingery paste and cook briefly before adding the oyster sauce, cornflour mixture and a few more drops of sesame oil.

Add the chicken pieces and cook again for 5 minutes, then add the tofu. Sprinkle with a generous amount of coriander, the spring onions and sesame seeds. If you like, drizzle with chilli oil.

GARLIC–MARINATED CHICKEN COOKED IN ALE WITH PARIS MASH

4 SERVES

1.6 kg (3 lb 8 oz) organic or good-quality
  chicken, cut into 12 pieces
90 ml (3 fl oz) extra virgin olive oil
2 brown onions, chopped
1 tablespoon chopped thyme
2 bay leaves
2 garlic cloves, finely chopped
250 ml (9 fl oz/1 cup) pale ale
500 ml (17 fl oz/2 cups) hot chicken stock
  (see page 133)

MARINADE

3 garlic cloves, peeled
1½ handfuls of flat-leaf (Italian) parsley
80 ml (2½ fl oz/⅓ cup) extra virgin
  olive oil

I don't think too many blokes could go past 'chicken braised in beer' if they saw it listed on a menu. I was lucky enough to be cooked this very dish on a trip to Tasmania. First I helped in the making of a batch of Cascade 'First Harvest' beer using freshly picked hops. After the beer was sorted, my fellow beer makers and I headed to Rodney Dunn's Agrarian Kitchen, which is a wonderful local cooking school that embraces ethical and sustainable farming of rare fruits, vegetables and animals. Rodney cooked some of his own farmed chicken in the previous year's 'First Harvest' beer. The result was chicken that melted off the bone into a beautiful sauce. This recipe is based on the one he cooked that day and it goes perfectly with buttery potato purée. The only thing you need to accompany it is a nice Tasmanian beer to drink with it. Cheers!

For the garlic and parsley marinade, place the garlic and parsley into a small blender and process until finely chopped, then add the oil and process to a paste.

Place the chicken pieces in a large bowl and season generously with sea salt.

Pour over the garlic and parsley marinade and rub into the chicken pieces. Cover and refrigerate for 3-4 hours.

Heat 60 ml (2 fl oz/¼ cup) of the olive oil in a large heavy-based roasting tin over medium-high heat. Add the chicken in batches and cook, turning occasionally, until golden brown. Remove the chicken pieces to a plate and set aside. Discard the oil from the tin, then scrape it clean and add the remaining oil. Gently sauté the onion, thyme, bay leaves and garlic over low-medium heat for about 20 minutes until the onion starts to brown.

PARIS MASH

1.25 kg (2 lb 12 oz) desiree potatoes, washed
 and unpeeled
100 ml (3½ fl oz) milk
220 ml (7½ fl oz) cream
180 g (6 oz) salted butter, at room
 temperature

Preheat the oven to 180°C (350°F/Gas 4). Increase the stovetop heat to high and return the chicken and any juices to the tin. When the juices are sizzling, add the beer and scrape the bottom of the tin with a wooden spoon. Allow the beer to bubble for 1 minute, then add the stock and bring to the boil. Cover with foil and cook in the oven for 30 minutes, then transfer back to the stovetop over low heat and cook for a further 30 minutes, or until the chicken is tender and almost falling off the bone. If the sauce has not reduced enough to coat the back of a spoon, remove the chicken from the tin and reduce the sauce further over medium heat. Season to taste.

Meanwhile, to make the mash, preheat the oven to 200°C (400°F/Gas 6). Tightly wrap each potato in foil and put on a baking tray, then place in the oven. Roast for about 40 minutes, or until tender when pierced with a skewer. Once the potatoes are very tender, use a kitchen cloth to hold the potatoes, then unwrap the foil and peel the skins while still hot.

Working in batches, pass the potatoes through a drum sieve or mouli straight into a saucepan.

Meanwhile, place the milk and cream in a separate saucepan and bring to the boil, then remove from the heat.

Stir the potatoes over low heat for 2 minutes, then slowly add the hot cream-milk mixture and butter while continuing to stir; once it has all been added, whip the potatoes with a wooden spoon until the mash starts to become nice and fluffy. Season with salt and freshly ground black pepper and serve immediately.

PAD KEE MAO

2 SERVES

250 g (9 oz) block of fresh thick rice
   noodles
2 tablespoons vegetable oil
2 tablespoons chopped garlic
2 tablespoons seeded and finely chopped
   bird's eye chillies
2 tablespoons fresh green peppercorns
   (optional)
200 g (7 oz) organic or good-quality
   chicken breast fillet, sliced
¼ bunch Chinese broccoli (gai larn), cut
   into 5 cm (2 inch) pieces
1 carrot, cut into 4 cm x 5 mm (1½ x
   ¼ inch) matchsticks
125 ml (4 fl oz/½ cup) water
1 tablespoon dark soy sauce
1½ tablespoons sweet soy sauce
1 tablespoon light soy sauce
2 teaspoons sugar
1 teaspoon fish sauce
1 tablespoon oyster sauce
2 free-range eggs
45 g (1½ oz/½ cup) bean sprouts, trimmed
½ cup holy basil leaves and flowers or
   Thai basil, picked
¼ teaspoon rice vinegar
lime halves, to serve

I try to visit Thailand every few years to get my fix of great food and beautiful beaches. It isn't hard to bring home a taste of Thailand. Pad kee mao is a personal favourite; it has everything you could want—heat from chilli, the aromatic flavour of holy basil and slippery fat noodles.

Gently separate the noodles by peeling them apart one at a time. Set aside.

Carefully add the oil to a hot wok over high heat and heat until the oil starts dancing around. Add the garlic, chilli and peppercorns, if using, stirring continuously so they don't burn.

When the garlic turns a light brown colour, add the chicken and cook, tossing constantly, for 15 seconds, then add the Chinese broccoli and carrot. Cook, stirring often, for about 1 minute. Add 80 ml (2½ fl oz/⅓ cup) of the water so the chicken and vegetables don't stick, then add the noodles and the remaining water and keep tossing for a further 1–2 minutes.

Add the soy sauces, sugar, fish sauce and oyster sauce and stir well. Push the noodles to one side of the wok and crack the eggs on the other bare side of the wok. Lightly scramble the eggs for 20 seconds, or until cooked, then toss the noodles with the eggs.

Add the bean sprouts, basil and vinegar and stir into the noodle mix. Once the basil has wilted it's ready. Serve with lime halves.

MEAT

PASTA WITH BACON, ROSEMARY, PINE MUSHROOMS AND POACHED EGG WITH BURNT BUTTER

4 SERVES

2 teaspoons olive oil
1 small onion
2 garlic cloves
10 slices of good-quality bacon, chopped
4 pine mushrooms, sliced
150 g (5½ oz) butter
1 tablespoon crème fraîche (optional)
500 g (1 lb 2 oz) fettuccine, pappardelle
   or linguine
2 teaspoons white wine vinegar
1 teaspoon salt
extra olive oil
4 free-range eggs
1 sprig of rosemary, finely chopped
50 g (1¾ oz/½ cup) shaved parmesan

Simple, simple, simple is how I would describe this dish, but it's simple with a touch of class. All the ingredients go together so well, and it really is a midweek superstar, where you can utilise some basic ingredients to please everyone in the house.

Heat the oil in a frying pan over low heat, add the onion and garlic and sauté for 5–10 minutes. Add the bacon, mushrooms and half the butter and continue to cook for a further 10 minutes, stirring regularly. When the mushrooms are cooked, add the crème fraîche and stir well.

Meanwhile, cook the pasta in a large saucepan of boiling salted water until al dente. Drain, then toss with a little oil and keep warm.

Fill a saucepan with water until approximately 10 cm (4 inches) deep. Add the vinegar and salt. Bring to the boil over medium-high heat, then reduce the heat to low-medium so the water starts to simmer. Crack one egg into a cup. Using a wooden spoon or a whisk stir the simmering water in one direction to form a whirlpool. Slide one egg in and cook for 3 minutes or until cooked to your liking. Remove the egg with a slotted spoon and sit on paper towel to soak up the excess water. Repeat with the remaining eggs.

While the eggs are poaching, add the pasta to the mushroom–bacon sauce and stir well so all of the pasta gets coated.

Divide the pasta evenly among four bowls. Return the frying pan to the heat and add the remaining butter. Allow this to foam up by swirling in the pan as it begins to bubble and turn a nut brown colour, then remove from the heat.

Using a slotted spoon, place one egg on top of each serving of pasta, then sprinkle each egg with the rosemary, parmesan and some pepper, then spoon over the burnt butter to finish.

MUM'S ASIAN-STYLE STICKY PORK SPARE RIBS

4 SERVES

MARINADE

12 garlic cloves, minced

2 long red chillies, finely chopped

250 ml (9 fl oz/1 cup) kecap manis

250 ml (9 fl oz/1 cup) light soy sauce

185 g (6½ oz/1 cup) soft brown sugar

80 ml (2½ fl oz/⅓ cup) fish sauce

125 ml (4 fl oz/½ cup) chicken stock
   (see page 133)

8 star anise

2 kg (4 lb 8 oz) pork ribs, cut Chinese-style
   (ask your butcher)

sesame seeds, toasted, to serve

If you have read my barbecue book, *My Grill*, you would have discovered and, I hope, cooked the Rum 'n' Coke ribs and the Maple syrup and tamarind glazed pork ribs. If you loved those recipes, then I'm sure you'll also love this one. I remember that as a kid Mum cooked ribs about once a month and I always got super excited—I loved the excuse to eat with my fingers and make a delicious mess all over my face.

To make the marinade, combine the garlic, chilli, kecap manis, soy sauce, sugar, fish sauce, stock and star anise in a large saucepan and bring to the boil. Set aside and allow to cool.

Once the marinade has cooled, add the ribs to the pan, turning to coat them in the marinade. Cover and refrigerate for 2 hours or, for great results, marinate overnight if time permits.

Preheat the oven to 190°C (375°F/Gas 5). Place the ribs and any marinade in a baking dish, cover with foil or a lid and roast for 30 minutes. Remove the foil or lid, turn the ribs and baste with the marinade. Cook for a further 30 minutes, or until caramelised and lightly charred.

Sprinkle with sesame seeds and serve with jasmine rice and steamed Asian vegetables.

KOREAN BEEF TARTARE

4 SERVES

6 garlic cloves, minced

80 ml (2½ fl oz/⅓ cup) soy sauce

2 tablespoons apple juice

1 tablespoon rice wine

1 tablespoon organic honey

2 teaspoons sesame oil

pinch of Korean chilli powder

600 g (1 lb 5 oz) beef fillet or sirloin, cut into strips

4 fresh free-range egg yolks

1 tablespoon toasted sesame seeds

2 tablespoons pine nuts, toasted

½ Lebanese (short) cucumber, sliced into matchsticks

1 nashi pear, sliced into matchsticks and placed into acidulated water with some sugar for 5 minutes (see Note)

3 tablespoons very thinly sliced spring onion (scallion)

1 tablespoon ssamjang (Korean fermented chilli bean paste) (optional)

8 witlof (chicory/Belgian endive) leaves

Raw meat is one of life's great luxuries and nowhere is it treated with more respect than in Asia—so many Asian meals call for thin slices of raw or just seared beef slices, sometimes briefly dipped into a hot broth to let the beef soak up the flavours. Here the focus is on perfectly raw beef. This is a delicious and very easy recipe to prepare either as a canapé with the mixture used as a filling for witlof leaves, or as a great start to an Asian feast. If you are not keen on the egg yolk sitting front and centre then mix it through the beef before serving. The best accompaniment is a cold Asian beer.

Combine the garlic with the soy sauce, apple juice, rice wine, honey, sesame oil, chilli powder, a pinch of sea salt and a little freshly ground black pepper, then mix it through the beef.

Divide the beef among four plates and make an indent in the top for the egg yolk. Add an egg yolk to each hole, then scatter the sesame seeds, pine nuts, cucumber, nashi pear and spring onion over the beef and egg, and drizzle with ssamjang, if you like. Serve with the witlof leaves on the side, which can be used as an edible scoop.

Note: Acidulated water is water with a little lemon juice or vinegar added; this will prevent the nashi pear becoming brown.

BO SSAM

1 kg (2 lb 4 oz) pork belly, skin scored
vegetable oil
2 butter lettuces, leaves separated
crisp-fried garlic (optional)
kimchi (Korean fermented vegetables)
   (optional)

SSAMJANG SAUCE
2 tablespoons hot chilli bean paste
2 spring onions (scallions), white part only,
   thinly sliced
1 tablespoon rice vinegar
1 tablespoon organic honey
1 small garlic clove
1 small knob of fresh ginger, finely grated

Ssam in Korean means 'wrapped', typically a dish of meat wrapped in lettuce or leafy vegetables. In this instance it is pork that is wrapped in lettuce leaves and served with the wonderful Korean sauce, ssamjang (fermented chilli bean paste). Here I have used pork belly and roasted it until it is golden and crispy but still has that gorgeous layer of unctuous fat under the skin and the wonderful meat that is so tender. I also like to serve it with some crisp-fried garlic and the Korean pickle, kimchi. This is a wonderful meal to serve a large group of people as it is a lot of fun to construct your own serving around the table.

Preheat the oven to 240°C (475°F/Gas 8) as you need to start by blasting the pork with heat.

Rub the pork with a little oil, then season with sea salt and place in a large roasting tin. Roast until the skin starts to bubble, about 30 minutes. Reduce the heat to 150°C (300°F/Gas 2) and continue to cook the pork belly for a further 2–2½ hours, or until tender. Remove from the oven and allow to rest.

To make the ssamjang sauce, combine all the ingredients in a bowl.

Thinly slice the pork belly and arrange on a platter with the lettuce cups, a bowl of the ssamjang sauce and, if you like, crisp-fried garlic and kimchi. Let your guests assemble their own lettuce cups.

MEATBALLS IN CHIPOTLE SAUCE WITH WARM TORTILLAS

4 SERVES

MEATBALLS

350 g (12 oz) minced (ground) pork
350 g (12 oz) minced (ground) beef
2 large free-range eggs
2 tablespoons dried oregano
2 teaspoons ground cumin
4 garlic cloves, minced
1 tablespoon flat-leaf (Italian) parsley,
    chopped
2 teaspoons salt
¼ teaspoon freshly ground black pepper

75 g (2½ oz/½ cup) plain (all-purpose) flour
2 tablespoons olive oil
4 flour tortillas, briefly warmed
coriander (cilantro) leaves, for garnish

CHIPOTLE SAUCE

1 tablespoon olive oil
1 brown onion, chopped
3 roma (plum) tomatoes, chopped
2 x 198 g (7 oz) tins chipotle chillies in
    adobo sauce (see Note)
1 teaspoon tomato paste (concentrated
    purée)
2 tablespoons organic honey
250 ml (9 fl oz/1 cup) chicken stock
    (see page 133)

SOUR CREAM SAUCE

125 g (4½ oz/½ cup) sour cream
1 teaspoon finely grated lime zest
3 teaspoons lime juice
pinch of salt and white pepper

The first restaurant I went to with my mates once I was of legal drinking age was a Mexican restaurant and it soon became a ritual for us to eat there every month. We loved the flavour and spiciness of the food but what made it fun was that we could share all the dishes and enjoy the obligatory margaritas. It was these spices and fun times that have kept me interested in Mexican cuisine and it's why I often make it in my kitchen at home. This is a lovely dish that will feed large groups with ease, so the next time you have a house full of guests, remember the Mexican food and the margaritas.

To make the meatballs, combine the pork and beef in a large bowl. Add the eggs, oregano, cumin, garlic, parsley, salt and pepper. Mix well with your hands until the ingredients are well incorporated.

To form the meatballs, place 1 tablespoon of the meat mixture in the palm of your hands and, moving both hands together in a circular motion, form a 3 cm (1¼ inch) ball. Set aside and repeat until you've used all the meat. Sprinkle the flour on a plate. Lightly coat the meatballs in the flour. Shake off any excess flour and set aside.

In a large saucepan, heat the oil over a medium–high heat. When the oil is hot, add the meatballs in batches. Seal the meatballs until golden, then remove from the pan. The meatballs don't need to be cooked through at this stage.

To make the chipotle sauce, combine the oil, onion, tomato, chipotle, tomato paste and honey in a blender and purée. Pour the mixture into the same saucepan that you used for the meatballs and bring up to the boil. Pour in the stock and bring back to the boil. Add the meatballs and cook for 10 minutes. They can stay in the sauce until ready to serve.

Meanwhile, mix all the ingredients for the sour cream sauce together.

Serve the meatballs on warm tortillas and scatter with coriander. Serve with the sour cream sauce.

Note: Chipotle chillies in adobo sauce are available at speciality food stores.

EGGPLANT AND PORK HOT POT

4 SERVES

300 g (10½ oz) minced (ground) pork
1 tablespoon light soy sauce
3 tablespoons Chinese rice wine
3 tablespoons peanut oil, for frying
3 garlic cloves, minced
4 cm (1½ inch) knob of fresh ginger, grated
3 tablespoons chilli bean paste
3 Japanese eggplants (aubergines), cut into
    large pieces
2 tablespoons water
375 g (13 oz) medium-sized fresh egg
    noodles
1½ tablespoons fish sauce
2 tablespoons cornflour (cornstarch),
    mixed with 2 tablespoons cold water
3 teaspoons dark soy sauce
200 ml (7 fl oz) chicken stock (see page 133)
2 teaspoons sugar
extra 125 ml (4 fl oz/½ cup) water
2 teaspoons sesame oil
coriander (cilantro) leaves, to serve

I love making this on a winter's night when I want some spice to warm me up. The slippery texture of the eggplant is wonderful, and this recipe shows that minced meat can be more than just a financially sound option, it can also be a delicious one.

Marinate the pork in the light soy sauce and half the Chinese rice wine. Set aside in the refrigerator until needed.

Preheat the oven to 180°C (350°F/Gas 4). Heat 2 tablespoons of the peanut oil in a frying pan over medium heat, then add half the garlic and ginger. Cook for about 1 minute, stirring constantly to make sure that the garlic does not burn. Add half the chilli bean paste to the pan and stir. Cook for a further 1 minute.

Add the eggplant to the pan, stir, then add the water and cover with a lid. Reduce the heat to low and cook for 8–10 minutes, shaking the pan occasionally to ensure the eggplant is coated with the chilli bean paste. Once the eggplant is partially cooked, remove it from the pan and drain on paper towel. Set aside.

Boil some water in a large saucepan and add the egg noodles. Cook, stirring occasionally, for 30 seconds. Drain the noodles and run under cold water. Set aside.

Meanwhile, add the remaining tablespoon of oil to the frying pan and cook the rest of the garlic and ginger for about 1 minute. Add the pork and cook for 5 minutes, or until the meat is cooked through but not dry. Stir in 2 teaspoons of the fish sauce. Set the pan aside.

Combine the cornflour mixture in a bowl, then pour into a small saucepan with the remaining 1 tablespoon of chilli bean paste and the remaining 1½ tablespoons of rice wine. Add the dark soy sauce, the remaining fish sauce, the stock, sugar and extra water. Stir well. Taste the sauce—you may need some more fish sauce depending on how salty you like it. Bring the sauce to the boil, whisking continuously, then set aside.

Add the noodles to a hot pot. Make a little well in the middle of the noodles and add the pork. Spoon the eggplant on top, then add the sauce. Sprinkle the sesame oil on top. Put the lid on firmly and pop the hot pot into the oven for 10 minutes. Garnish with coriander.

EVIL HOT LAMB

4 SERVES

SPICE MIX
5 star anise
3 dried bay leaves
2 teaspoons sichuan peppercorns

600 g (1 lb 5 oz) lamb backstrap or loin
    fillet, fat removed, sliced into long,
    thin strips
1 teaspoon salt
1 teaspoon freshly ground black pepper
2 tablespoons sweet paprika
80 ml (2½ fl oz/⅓ cup) water
50 ml (1½ fl oz) vegetable oil
1 brown onion, sliced
½ red capsicum (pepper), seeds removed
    and sliced
½ bunch of spring onions (scallions), cut
    into 6 cm (2½ inch) pieces
7 bird's eye chillies, seeds removed and
    thinly sliced
250 ml (9 fl oz/1 cup) salt-reduced chicken
    stock
3 teaspoons chilli flakes
2½ tablespoons sugar
1 teaspoon garlic powder
2 teaspoons cornflour (cornstarch), mixed
    with 1½ tablespoons water
2 tablespoons chilli oil (optional)

Recently I took the kids up to the mid-north coast of New South Wales on a surfing holiday. We stayed in a caravan park and as it had minimal cooking facilities, we headed into the local town, Forster, for some Chinese food. I love the varied nature of the local Chinese restaurants you find throughout Australia— sometimes they are disappointing and other times, such as this time, I come away pleasantly surprised. I always order something off the chef's list of recommendations. On this occasion, one recipe stood out, simply titled 'Evil hot lamb'. The dish lived up to its name and it was so hot that my mate, Donnie, and I struggled to eat it, but we enjoyed every painful mouthful. I have since cooked it at home but I have toned down the chilli component. If you love chilli then increase the quantity or leave in the seeds.

To make the spice mix, heat a wok or frying pan over medium heat, add the star anise, bay leaves and peppercorns and stir for 3 minutes until fragrant. Transfer to a spice grinder or use a mortar and pestle and process or pound until the mixture forms a powder. Set aside.

Put the sliced meat, salt, pepper and paprika in a bowl and mix well. Add the water and marinate for 15 minutes.

Heat a wok or large frying pan over medium–high heat and heat the oil. Once the oil is hot, add the lamb with the liquid and stir-fry for 1 minute. Add the onion, capsicum, spring onion and sliced chilli and stir-fry until lightly golden, then remove from the wok and set aside in a dish.

Pour the chicken stock into the wok; add the chilli flakes, sugar, garlic powder and 2 teaspoons of the spice mix. Bring to the boil, return the lamb and cooked vegetables to the wok and toss well for 1 minute until boiling. Add the cornflour mixture to the lamb. Cook until it starts to thicken. Place the lamb and vegetables on a serving plate and pour chilli oil, if using, around and on top of the meat. Serve with steamed rice or your favourite type of Asian noodles.

MARINADE

1 litre (35 fl oz/4 cups) dry white wine
2 tablespoons extra virgin olive oil
250 ml (9 fl oz/1 cup) chicken stock
  (see page 133)
2 red onions, sliced
150 g (5½ oz) semi-dried (sun-blushed)
  tomatoes, chopped
4 bay leaves
½ bunch of thyme, chopped
½ bunch of sage, chopped

1 lamb shoulder on the bone 1.5–2 kg
  (3 lb 5 oz–4 lb 8 oz), cut into three pieces
1 tablespoon olive oil
2 lemons, cut in half
75 g (2½ oz/1 cup) shredded white cabbage
  (optional)
60 g (2¼ oz) chopped butter
500 g (1 lb 2 oz) rigatoni
1 bunch of flat-leaf (Italian) parsley, finely
  shredded
freshly grated pecorino, to serve

LAMB RAGU WITH RIGATONI

This dish is based on one that was cooked for me by two amazing Italian cooks, Daniela and Stefania, on the television show, *My Kitchen Rules*. They cooked marinated baby goat with braised cabbage and roasted kipfler potatoes—it was so moreish and flavoursome that I had a smile from ear to ear. This recipe is based on theirs but I have changed the goat to lamb. Thank-you for the inspiration, girls!

To make the marinade, combine the wine, extra virgin olive oil, stock, onion, tomato, bay leaves, thyme, sage and some salt and freshly ground black pepper in a large non-reactive bowl.

Add the lamb pieces to the marinade and marinate for a minimum of 2 hours, preferably overnight if time permits.

Preheat the oven to 150°C (300°F/Gas 2). Drain the meat and onion from the marinade, reserving the liquid.

Heat the olive oil in a flameproof casserole dish over medium-high heat until smoking. Add the meat and turn occasionally for 3–5 minutes until browned. Add the onion to the casserole dish and sauté for 10–12 minutes until starting to caramelise. Add the remaining marinade to the casserole dish. Squeeze over the juice from the lemons and add the lemon halves to the casserole dish. Bring to the boil.

Cover tightly with baking paper, cover with a lid and bake for 1½ hours, then remove the lemons. Add the cabbage, if using, and continue cooking for a further 1–1½ hours until the meat is tender and almost falls from the bone. You may need to add a little water as you are cooking if the liquid reduces too much.

Remove the lamb pieces and bay leaves from the sauce and, when cool enough to handle, break the meat into bite-sized pieces, discarding the bones. Skim off and discard the oil, then return the meat to the sauce. Mix in the butter and season with salt and freshly ground black pepper.

Meanwhile, cook the pasta in a large saucepan of boiling salted water until al dente. Drain. Add the lamb liquor to the pasta, then fold in the meat and most of the parsley. Top with grated pecorino and the remaining parsley.

BUCATINI WITH CHILLI AND PANCETTA

4 SERVES

1 tablespoon extra virgin olive oil

1 red onion, cut in half lengthways, then sliced into 5 mm (¼ inch) wide pieces

3 garlic cloves, sliced

1½ teaspoons chilli flakes

350 g (12 oz) thinly sliced pancetta or good-quality bacon

500 g (1 lb 2 oz/2 cups) ready-made tomato pasta sauce

500 g (1 lb 2 oz) bucatini

2 tablespoons finely shredded flat-leaf (Italian) parsley

freshly grated pecorino, to serve

I spent a number of years of my apprenticeship working in Italian restaurants where I learned the finer details of making my own pasta and how to make the traditional pasta sauces. One of the most important lessons was learning how much sauce to pair with the pasta—a lot of people get it wrong and drown the pasta with sauce, when the sauce should only just coat the pasta and not overpower it. My favourite tomato-based pasta sauce is the classic amatriciana, a combination of pork, chilli, tomato, garlic and parsley tossed with bucatini, which is a thick type of hollow spaghetti. If you are cooking for more that six people I would suggest you swap the bucatini for penne, rigatoni or orrechiette.

Combine the oil, onion, garlic, chilli flakes and pancetta in a large frying pan and cook over low heat for about 12 minutes until the onion is soft and the pancetta has rendered much of its fat. Drain most of the fat out of the pan. Add the tomato sauce, turn up the heat and bring to the boil, then reduce the heat to a simmer and allow to bubble for 6–7 minutes.

Meanwhile, cook the bucatini in a large saucepan of boiling salted water until not quite al dente, but still firm. Drain.

Add the pasta and parsley to the simmering sauce and toss for about 1 minute to coat. Divide among four heated bowls and serve immediately, topped with freshly grated pecorino.

LAMB SHANK PIE

4 SERVES

4 lamb shanks, trimmed
2 tablespoons olive oil
3 carrots, chopped
3 brown onions, chopped
4 celery stalks, chopped
½ celeriac, cut into 3 cm (1¼ inch) chunks
2 large potatoes, diced
2 tablespoons plain (all-purpose) flour
400 g (14 oz) tin whole peeled tomatoes
550 ml (19 fl oz) good-quality red wine
100 g (3½ oz/⅔ cup) peas
⅓ cup chopped flat-leaf (Italian) parsley
375 g (13 oz) block of puff pastry
1 free-range egg, whisked with
   1 tablespoon water

I can't think of anything better than to combine Australia's number one meat, lamb, with our favourite dish, the meat pie. To make a great meat pie you need to pick your cut of meat carefully—you want something that benefits from long, slow braising and in my opinion it has to be the shank. This pie does take some time to cook so plan well in advance and you can freeze any leftover mixture for a later time.

Season the lamb shanks with salt and pepper. Heat half the oil in a saucepan or flameproof casserole dish over medium heat, then brown the lamb shanks on all sides until evenly browned. Transfer to a warm plate and drain off any excess oil.

Heat the remaining oil in the pan and add the carrot, onion, celery, celeriac and potato. Increase the heat to high and, as the vegetables begin to soften, reduce the heat to medium and cook for 15 minutes, stirring occasionally. Add half the flour and stir again so the vegetables are coated.

Meanwhile, put the tomatoes in a blender with the wine and remaining flour, then blitz until combined.

Add the tomato liquid to the pan and stir well. Return the shanks and any juices to the pan—it's fine if the bones stick out a bit but the meat section of the shank should be submerged. Add the peas. Place a lid on the pan and simmer gently for 2 hours over low heat. When the lamb shanks are cooked, lift them out of the pan with tongs, cool slightly and remove the meat from the bones, reserving the bones if you like. Shred the meat loosely and pour a small amount of the cooking liquor on top to keep it moist.

Return the pan to the stovetop, increase the heat and simmer the vegetables and sauce for 10-20 minutes, or until the sauce reduces. Remove from the heat, return the shank meat to the pan, add the parsley and season with salt and pepper. Set aside to cool. Preheat the oven to 180°C (350°F/Gas 4).

Transfer the mixture to a 2.5 litre (10 cup) ovenproof ceramic dish. Roll out the pastry on a lightly floured surface until about 3 mm (⅛ inch) thick and trim to the size of your dish, allowing an extra 3 cm (1¼ inches) all around. Place on top of the dish. Cut several slits in the top of the pastry for steam to escape while cooking and, if you like, carefully insert the bones through the slits. Turn the overlapping edges of the pastry under and crimp all around the casserole dish, ensuring the pastry is tightly secured. Brush lightly with the egg wash, then bake for 40 minutes, or until golden.

HEALTHY SMOKED HOCK COMFORT SOUP

4 SERVES

3 tablespoons olive oil
1 large brown onion, diced
3 garlic cloves, sliced
700 g (1 lb 9 oz) smoked ham hock
140 g (5 oz/1 cup) chopped celery (about 3 stalks)
130 g (4½ oz/1 cup) chopped parsnip
155 g (5½ oz/1 cup) chopped carrot
½ leek, white part only, sliced
200 g (7 oz/1 cup) fresh or tinned corn kernels
220 g (7¾ oz/1 cup) pearl barley
220 g (7¾ oz/1 cup) Italian-style soup mix (dried peas, lentils and beans)
4 litres (16 cups) water
1 bunch of flat-leaf (Italian) parsley, chopped
2 tablespoons chopped rosemary

My mother-in-law, Poldi, has been making this soup for my kids ever since they started eating solids. It is one of their favourite meals, which makes me so happy as it is packed full of healthy vegetables. The key to getting kids to eat vegetables is to start them off early and to incorporate vegetables into as much of your cooking as possible. It's also important for kids to learn where vegetables and fruit come from. I know from experience what a difference this can make to their attitude towards vegetables as my kids only started eating tomatoes when they could pick them off the vine themselves. If your kids are fussy then try this soup and I think you'll have the same success that we did. Make a big batch as it freezes well, so you will always have a nutritious meal on hand.

Heat the oil in a stockpot over low–medium heat, add the onion and garlic and cook gently until golden.

Add the ham hock, celery, parsnip, carrot, leek, corn, barley, soup mix and water to the pot. Bring up to the boil, then reduce to a simmer and cook for 2 hours. Remove the ham hock from the pan and remove the fat part. Chop the lean meat into pieces and return to the soup. Cook for a further 1 hour.

Add the parsley and rosemary, then serve with a crusty bread roll or sourdough.

POLENTA WITH SAUSAGE, PORK BELLY AND MUSHROOMS

4 SERVES

6 thick Italian pork sausages (100% pork)

500 g (1 lb 2 oz) pork belly, cut into large, thick slices

2 bay leaves

250 ml (9 fl oz/1 cup) white vinegar

generous slug of extra virgin olive oil

1 onion, finely minced

1 carrot, finely minced

1 celery stalk, finely chopped

125 ml (4 fl oz/½ cup) dry white wine

1 garlic clove, finely minced (optional)

2 tablespoons tomato paste (concentrated purée)

2 x 500 ml (17 fl oz) bottles of Italian tomato passata or ready-made tomato pasta sauce

2 teaspoons sugar

250 ml (9 fl oz/1 cup) hot water

300 g (10½ oz) Swiss brown mushrooms, roughly chopped

freshly grated parmesan, to serve

POLENTA

750 ml (26 fl oz/3 cups) water

150 g (5½ oz/1 cup) polenta

1 teaspoon salt

I recently received an email from a woman called Rina Valerio who generously wanted to share her family's recipe for pork and mushroom ragu on soft polenta. I've cooked it at home and it's so good that I have to share it with you.

Place the sausages and pork belly in a large saucepan, cover with cold water and add the bay leaves and vinegar. Bring to the boil and boil for about 10 minutes—this will get rid of the strong porky smell. Remove the meats from the pan, cut the sausages into large pieces and, if you like, cut the pork into smaller pieces.

Heat the oil in a saucepan, add the onion, carrot and celery and gently sauté for 5 minutes. Add the meats and gently sauté for a further 10 minutes before adding the wine. Cook until all the wine has evaporated. Add the garlic, if using, and tomato paste and gently cook for a couple more minutes, then add the tomato passata, sugar and some salt and pepper. When the sauce comes to the boil, reduce to a gentle simmer, add the hot water and simmer gently for at least 1–1½ hours, slightly covered.

Meanwhile, to make the polenta, pour the water into a saucepan and bring to almost boiling point; do not let the water boil, as polenta will go lumpy when added to boiling water. Remove the pan from the heat and add the polenta in a thin stream, stirring constantly. Return the pan to the stovetop, reduce the heat to a simmer, season with salt and cook for at least 1 hour, stirring the polenta frequently while keeping the top partially covered with a lid to protect yourself from the polenta, which can spit.

About 30 minutes prior to the polenta being ready, add the mushrooms to the sauce, cover again with a lid and cook for a further 30 minutes.

When you are ready to serve the polenta, pour it into a large serving bowl or onto the traditional serving container, a wooden board, or divide among individual plates. Cover with a generous amount of the sauce and top with grated parmesan.

MA PO TOFU WITH LAU'S HOME-MADE SPICY MA PO SAUCE

4 SERVES

MA PO SAUCE

1 large red capsicum (pepper), seeds
   removed and sliced
2 teaspoons water
2 tablespoons dried salted black beans
3 teaspoons vegetable oil
1 teaspoon dried red peppercorns or
   sichuan peppercorns
5 garlic cloves
3 pieces of dried shallot
½ small onion, diced
6 fresh bird's eye chillies, diced
6 dried red chillies, soaked in water until
   softened, then diced
extra 100 ml (3½ fl oz) vegetable oil
3 tablespoons white miso paste
2 tablespoons oyster sauce
3 tablespoons sugar
2 teaspoons salt

I've loved Ma po tofu, or Grandma's tofu, for years. I think this is one of the best ways to eat tofu and that this dish will convert tofu haters into tofu lovers. The tofu carries the other flavours of the dish and softens them not only through the subtleness of the tofu flavour but also with its silky texture. I am lucky to have been graciously given this recipe by Gilbert Lau, the grandfather of Cantonese cuisine in Australia (think the Flower Drum and Lau's Family Kitchen, both in Victoria). There are a few legends about the origins of the name of this dish: one centres on the translation for ma po, which means 'old woman with pock marks'. Legend states that a pock-marked old woman would serve this dish to poor traders. Whatever the real reason for the name, I love the taste and I believe you will too. The recipe is quite long, but please persevere as I think this is one of the best recipes in the book.

To make the ma po sauce, blend the capsicum with the water until it becomes a purée. Soak the black beans in some water for 15 minutes, then drain.

   Heat the oil in a wok and fry the peppercorns until fragrant. Drain, then use a mortar and pestle to finely grind them. Transfer to a plate. Use a mortar and pestle to finely grind the garlic, dried shallot, onion, and fresh and dried chilli, keeping this mixture separate from the ground peppercorns.

MARINADE

1 teaspoon potato flour or cornflour
    (cornstarch)
pinch of salt
½ teaspoon sugar
pinch of ground white pepper
1 tablespoon vegetable oil
2 tablespoons water

200 g (7 oz) minced (ground) pork
500 g (1 lb 2 oz) packet of silken tofu
2 tablespoons vegetable oil
2 garlic cloves, very finely chopped
½ teaspoon minced fresh ginger
2 dried shiitake mushrooms, soaked for
    30 minutes, stalks removed, diced
20 g (¾ oz) sichuan preserved vegetable,
    rinsed, drained and finely chopped
1 tablespoon Chinese rice wine
180–200 ml (5¾–7 fl oz) chicken stock (see
    page 133) or water
2 teaspoons oyster sauce
1 teaspoon sugar
¼ teaspoon salt
1 teaspoon dark soy sauce
1 tablespoon potato flour or cornflour
    (cornstarch), mixed with 2 tablespoons
    water
½ spring onion (scallion), green part only,
    shredded

Heat 2 tablespoons of the extra oil in the wok until just smoking. Add the ground garlic mixture and stir-fry over low heat until fragrant. Add the soaked black beans, miso paste and the remaining 3 tablespoons of oil, 1 tablespoon at a time, and stir-fry the mixture until it combines well.

Add the capsicum purée, oyster sauce, sugar and salt and stir for another 5 minutes; lastly, add the ground peppercorns. Set aside 2–3 tablespoons of the sauce, and store the remaining sauce in a sterilised jar for future use. It can be kept in the refrigerator for up to 6 months.

To make the marinade, combine the ingredients in a bowl. Add the pork to the marinade and stand for 15 minutes.

Cut the tofu into 2.5 cm (1 inch) cubes and soak in a bowl of hot water for 4 minutes. Drain.

Heat the oil in the wok over high heat and stir-fry the pork until approximately 80 percent cooked. Reduce the heat to medium, add the garlic, ginger, soaked and diced mushroom, preserved vegetable, rice wine, stock and 2–3 tablespoons of the ma po sauce and stir for 20 seconds. Carefully add the tofu, oyster sauce, sugar, salt and soy sauce and simmer for 1–1½ minutes, or until the tofu has absorbed the flavours. Stir in the potato flour or cornflour mixture and cook until the sauce is slightly thickened. Transfer to a serving dish, sprinkle with spring onion and serve with steamed brown rice.

MINUTE STEAK WITH ANCHOVY BUTTER

2–4 SERVES

ANCHOVY BUTTER

7 large anchovies, finely chopped
1 tablespoon lemon juice
160 g (5¾ oz) butter, softened
2 garlic cloves, minced
2 tablespoons chopped flat-leaf (Italian)
    parsley

4 x 120 g (4¼ oz) minute steaks
50 ml (1½ fl oz) olive oil

This is a great dish to cook over a campfire or when you are on holidays. It only takes a few minutes to prepare and then to cook. I know a recipe like this doesn't really need much explaining as it is pretty straightforward, but this book is about what I like to cook and eat at home (and also on holiday) so I thought I'd better sneak it in here. The key to this recipe is to buy great quality butter and, of course, anchovies and steak— please don't skimp on quality as it will show in the final dish, and really you should treat yourself to the best. Ideally this is served with crispy fries or roasted potatoes, a crisp salad and cold beer. If you aren't particularly fond of anchovies, then just make a lovely herb and garlic butter or replace the anchovies with chilli flakes for a bit of added spice.

To make the anchovy butter, place the anchovies, lemon juice, butter, garlic and parsley in a food processor and blend until all combined. Continue to blend while adding salt and pepper to taste. Transfer to a bowl and leave at room temperature to allow it to melt perfectly on the steak when serving.

To cook the steak, heat a frying pan over medium–high heat. Before adding the meat to the pan, season the steaks with salt and pepper and drizzle them with oil.

Place the steaks on the hot pan and cook for 30 seconds on one side or until golden, then turn over and cook until golden again. Remove from the heat and serve with a dollop of anchovy butter on top and a garden salad on the side.

MY CHINESE SPAGHETTI BOLOGNESE

2 SERVES

50 g (1¾ oz) shredded dried black wood ear fungus

1 bunch of spring onions (scallions), chopped

2 tablespoons grapeseed oil

8 garlic cloves, chopped

3 tablespoons minced fresh ginger

100 g (3½ oz) shiitake mushroom, sliced

400 g (14 oz) minced (ground) beef

80 ml (2½ fl oz/⅓ cup) Chinese rice wine

2–4 tablespoons yellow chilli bean paste or sauce

80 ml (2½ fl oz/⅓ cup) light soy sauce

3 tablespoons Chinese black vinegar

250 ml (9 fl oz/1 cup) chicken stock (see page 133)

500 g (1 lb 2 oz) hokkien noodles

155 g (5½ oz/1 cup) podded soya beans or peas

100 g (3½ oz) water chestnuts, sliced

1 handful of coriander (cilantro) leaves, to garnish

1 long red chilli, seeds removed and finely chopped, to garnish

We all love a dish that is no-nonsense, inexpensive and has only a few ingredients. I would recommend that you use the best possible meat for this meal and feel free to jazz it up with any vegetables you like. This isn't a recipe to win over friends, it is just a simple one I like to make at home when I don't have a lot of time, but I want a lot of flavour. I especially love the way the Chinese black vinegar gives a lovely sharpness to the dish.

Place the wood ear fungus in a large heatproof bowl and cover with boiling water. Set aside for 30 minutes, or until rehydrated. Slice and set aside.

Cook off the spring onion in the oil in a wok over high heat, add the garlic, ginger and shiitake mushrooms, then add the beef. Cook the beef for 2–3 minutes, or until cooked through, then add the rice wine; when the alcohol is cooked off, add the yellow bean paste, soy sauce, vinegar and wood ear fungus. Add the stock and continue to cook for 10–15 minutes.

Place the hokkien noodles in a bowl and pour over boiling water. Drain and add to the wok along with the soya beans or peas and water chestnuts; stir through the meat. Cook for 2 minutes, or until heated through. Top with the coriander and chilli.

SHANGHAI-STYLE PORK SPARE RIBS

4 SERVES

SAUCE

250 ml (9 fl oz/1 cup) Chinese black
  vinegar
220 g (7¾ oz/1 cup) caster (superfine) sugar
1 tablespoon soy sauce
1 tablespoon grated fresh ginger
1 tablespoon minced garlic
2 tablespoon salt

1.5–2 litres (6–8 cups) vegetable oil, for
  deep-frying
1.5 kg (3 lb 5 oz) American-style pork
  spareribs (2 full racks), cut into
  individual ribs
extra 1 tablespoon vegetable oil
1 tablespoon sesame seeds, toasted

Ribs are always a crowd pleaser and better still are so easy to prepare. It is a good idea to serve a salad or vegetables with ribs to help cut through their richness.

Preheat the oven to 160°C (315°F/Gas 2–3). Combine the vinegar, sugar, soy sauce, ginger, garlic and salt in a bowl and set aside.

Pour the oil into a medium-large saucepan and heat the oil to about 180°C (350°F). Cut the ribs into individual ribs. Add the ribs to the oil in batches, about eight at a time, and cook for 5–8 minutes, or until golden. Drain on paper towel and set to one side.

Heat the extra oil in a wok, add the sauce and stir until the sugar has dissolved.

Put the ribs in a roasting tin or deep ovenproof dish and pour the sauce over them, then toss until the ribs are covered in the mixture. Cover with foil and roast for 1 hour. Carefully drain the liquid into a saucepan and reduce the liquid over medium heat until it becomes syrupy. Toss the sauce with the ribs and return to the oven for a further 10 minutes. Place the ribs in a serving dish and sprinkle with sesame seeds.

VEAL SALTIMBOCCA

4 SERVES

ONION CONFIT
155 g (5½ oz/1 cup) chopped brown onion
250 ml (9 fl oz/1 cup) olive oil

8 x 80 g (2¾ oz) pieces of veal backstrap
16 sage leaves, 8 left whole, the rest
   thinly sliced
8 slices of prosciutto
plain (all-purpose) flour, for dusting
2 tablespoons olive oil
2 tablespoons onion confit (see recipe
   above)
250 ml (9 fl oz/1 cup) dry white wine
100 g (3½ oz) unsalted butter, chopped

When I was an apprentice on the Gold Coast, Queensland, I worked in an Italian restaurant for a year. I was thrilled to be a first-year apprentice who was allowed to cook rather than just do the dishes and this was my favourite dish to prepare. Because I'd been thrown in at the deep end, I tried to make each and every saltimbocca perfect by giving it all my attention. And today I still put 100 percent effort into everything I cook, whether it is simply toasting a piece of bread for my kids or using caviar and foie gras at work. As for the saltimbocca, I have a soft spot for the dish, and so I do cook it at home from time to time. And with it, I love to serve some cavolo nero, spinach or broccolini that has been sautéed with a touch of garlic and lemon.

To make the onion confit, place the onion and olive oil in a small saucepan and place over the lowest heat possible on your stovetop. Cook for 2 hours or until the onion is soft (you do not want the oil boiling—it should be just past warm).

Bash out the veal with a meat mallet into even-sized pieces. Season with salt and pepper, place one sage leaf on top then a piece of prosciutto, then secure with a toothpick.

Dust the veal lightly in flour then pan-fry in the oil in a large frying pan over medium heat until golden on one side. Turn and cook the other side until golden. Add the onion confit and deglaze the pan with the wine, then add the sliced sage. Add the butter and some salt and pepper and cook until you have a good sauce consistency.

LAMB MEATBALLS WITH TOMATO AND CORIANDER

SAUCE

1 tablespoon vegetable oil
1 brown onion, chopped
1 garlic clove, finely chopped
1 bunch of coriander (cilantro) leaves
    and roots, washed and chopped (about
    100 g/3½ oz dry leaves)
½ bunch of spring onions (scallions),
    finely chopped (about 100 g/3½ oz)
1 kg (2 lb 4 oz) ripe tomatoes (roma/plum
    tomatoes are good), roughly chopped
1 teaspoon freshly ground black pepper
2 tablespoons grated palm sugar (jaggery)
3 tablespoons fish sauce
1 teaspoon seeded and chopped red chilli

MEATBALLS

1 kg (2 lb 4 oz) minced (ground) lamb
    (not too lean)
3 red Asian shallots, minced
1 teaspoon minced garlic
2 tablespoons sugar
1½ teaspoons salt
½ teaspoon freshly ground black pepper
2 spring onions (scallions), white part only,
    finely minced
225 g (8 oz) tin chopped water chestnuts,
    rinsed and drained

vegetable oil
3 fresh baguettes, cut in half widthways,
    then cut open lengthways
sliced red chilli, to serve

My good friends Nhut and Jeremy own a little restaurant in Sydney called Snakebean. To say that the boys are a bit flamboyant would be an understatement—I love their energy and the way they live their life ... it is always a lot of fun to be around them and there is never a dull moment in their restaurant. Nhut is Vietnamese and he is an amazing chef who uses well balanced and addictive flavours. He has graciously shared one of his signature recipes here and I am sure you will love it as much as I do. Make extra as the meatballs are delicious in a baguette or bread roll the next day.

To make the sauce, heat the oil in a large heavy-based frying pan. Sauté the onion and garlic until the onion is translucent. Add the coriander, spring onion, tomato and pepper and stir. Simmer for 5 minutes before adding the palm sugar, fish sauce and chilli. Simmer for a further 15 minutes.

To make the meatballs, mix all the ingredients together in a large bowl. Rub a little vegetable oil on your hands, then form golf ball-sized meatballs.

Either bake the meatballs in the oven at 180°C (350°F/Gas 4) for 15–20 minutes then add to the sauce or, once the sauce is cooked, carefully add the raw meatballs and cook over low heat for 30 minutes. Shake the pan rather than stirring to avoid breaking up the balls.

To serve, carefully lift out the meatballs and place them in the baguette, then ladle the sauce over the meatballs. Garnish with coriander and sliced chilli.

BARBECUED SIRLOIN WITH MINT, CHILLI, LEMON AND ROCKET

4 SERVES

4 x 220 g (7¾ oz) trimmed sirloin steaks
vegetable oil
1 long red chilli, seeds removed
½ bunch of mint, leaves picked
¼ bunch of oregano, leaves picked
1 lemon
100 ml (3½ fl oz) extra virgin olive oil
2 handfuls of rocket (arugula) leaves
balsamic vinegar

In my opinion, the eye fillet is the least attractive piece of meat and I very rarely use it unless I am serving it raw because its low fat content means it lacks flavour. The sirloin on the other hand is the opposite: it has a wonderful fat content and far superior flavour which means it can stand up to strong flavours such as mint, chilli and lemon. The important thing to remember when you are cooking any type of meat is to bring it to room temperature before you cook it so that you don't shock the meat and make it tense up. Play around with different spices and seasonings for your steaks, but this is a classic Italian combination that hits just the right note.

Take the steaks out of the refrigerator and allow them to come to room temperature.

Preheat the barbecue hotplate or chargrill to high. Brush the steaks with a little oil and cook for about 4–5 minutes each side until they are rare to medium-rare, then remove from the heat and allow to rest for 5 minutes.

On a large clean chopping board, finely chop the chilli, followed by the herbs so they all combine together as one. Spread this herby mixture out over the board and season with salt and pepper.

Coat the steaks with the herb mixture, a squeeze of lemon juice and half the oil so the steak becomes dressed with the herbs. Slice the meat into thick strips.

Toss the rocket with the remaining oil and the vinegar, then place it on top of the steaks and serve.

SLOW-ROASTED SHOULDER OF PORK WITH CARROTS AND CRACKLING

6 SERVES

1 tablespoon fennel seeds

3 large garlic cloves, peeled

2–3 kg (4 lb 8 oz–6 lb 12 oz) trimmed pork shoulder roast, bone in (ask your butcher to score the rind)

6 large carrots (about 1 kg/2 lb 4 oz)

500 ml (17 fl oz/2 cups) hot chicken stock (see page 133)

1 litre (4 cups) hot water

There is nothing more satisfying than a roast that has been cooked slowly for hours. Any piece of meat, whether it be beef, lamb, goat or pork is absolutely mouthwatering when the meat starts to fall away from the bone and melt in the mouth. I love slow cooking, but it does require some forward planning. This is a very basic recipe that really lets the produce speak for itself, so try to source the very best pork and carrots that you can.

Pound the fennel seeds and garlic using a mortar and pestle—the mixture can be a bit chunky. Season lightly with salt and pepper.

Rub the garlic mixture over the pork meat, not the rind. Place the pork in a shallow dish, rind side down, cover, then refrigerate for several hours or overnight if time permits.

Preheat the oven to 140°C (275°F/Gas 1). Place the pork in a baking dish, rind side up. Add the carrots, stock and water. Cover the dish tightly with at least two layers of foil, keeping it sealed so no steam can escape. Roast the pork for 6 hours. To check if it is ready, see if the meat pulls away easily from the bone. If there is any resistance, it needs to be cooked for a little longer.

Increase the oven temperature to 220°C (425°F/Gas 7). Peel the rind away from the pork. Cover the pork meat and keep in a warm place. Put the rind on a clean baking tray and return to the oven for 20 minutes, or until the rind has bubbled and is crisp. Roughly chop the crackling.

Meanwhile, set the carrots aside on a warm plate. Strain the pan juices through muslin (cheesecloth) or a fine sieve, then set aside.

Remove any fat or bones from the pork. Shred the meat coarsely with two forks. Place in a bowl and stir through the reserved pan juices. Serve the pork with the carrots and crackling.

BEEF RENDANG (RENDANG DAGING) OR SPICY BEEF STEW WITH COCONUT

4 SERVES

SPICE PASTE

5 red Asian shallots, peeled

2.5 cm (1 inch) knob of fresh galangal, peeled

3 lemongrass stems, white part only

5 garlic cloves, peeled

2.5 cm (1 inch) knob of fresh ginger, peeled

10–12 dried red chillies, soaked in warm water for 20 minutes and seeds removed

2 teaspoons tamarind pulp

100 ml (3½ fl oz) vegetable oil

1 cinnamon stick (about 5 cm/2 inches long)

3 whole cloves

3 star anise

3 cardamom pods

700 g (1 lb 9 oz) boneless beef short ribs (cut into 3–4 cm/1¼–1½ inch cubes)

1 lemongrass stem, cut into 10 cm (4 inch) lengths and pounded

250 ml (9 fl oz/1 cup) thick coconut cream

250 ml (9 fl oz/1 cup) water

6 kaffir lime leaves, very thinly sliced

6 tablespoons toasted coconut

1 tablespoon sugar or grated palm sugar (jaggery), or to taste

extra coconut cream, to serve

2 tablespoons crisp-fried shallots or onions

This is my favourite version of the popular Malaysian dish, beef rendang. There is a bit of work involved as you do have to make the spice mix, toast the coconut and cook the beef slowly, but you will be very well rewarded with the smiles of your friends and family, not to mention with your own sense of satisfaction. I use beef short ribs as I love cooking meat on the bone, but you can just as easily use any stewing beef. This stew only gets better with time, so try making it a day or two before you want to serve it.

To make the spice paste, chop the ingredients then blend in a food processor until finely chopped.

Soak the tamarind pulp in warm water. Strain through a sieve, reserving the juice and discarding the seeds. Set aside.

Heat the oil in a heavy-based saucepan, add the spice paste, cinnamon, cloves, star anise and cardamom and stir-fry until fragrant. Add the beef and the pounded lemongrass and stir for 1 minute. Add the coconut cream, tamarind liquid and water and bring to a simmer over medium heat. Add the kaffir lime leaves, coconut and sugar, then stir well.

Reduce the heat to low, cover with a lid and simmer for 1–1½ hours, or until the meat is really tender. Remove the lid and simmer for 30–40 minutes, or until the liquid has reduced to a sauce consistency. Add salt to taste. If not sweet enough, add more sugar to taste. Serve immediately, topped with a drizzle of coconut cream and crisp-fried shallots or onions.

SIDE DISHES

03

WALDORF SALAD

VINAIGRETTE
3 teaspoons dijon mustard
1½ tablespoons good-quality red wine
  vinegar
80 ml (2½ fl oz/⅓ cup) canola oil
2 teaspoons plain yoghurt

4 fuji apples
½ celery stalk, julienned, and picked leaves
juice of 1 lemon
100 g (3½ oz) toasted walnuts
2 witlofs (chicory/Belgian endives),
  leaves separated

I was lucky enough to stay in the majestic Waldorf Astoria hotel on my first visit to New York City a few years ago. I was there for 2 weeks in preparation for cooking for a fund-raising dinner for 300 guests. I fell in love with New York and the buzz of the city; it was like Sydney on steroids. Anything you wanted you got the best—sushi, Mexican, fine dining, hot dogs. Every night I would end up back at the Waldorf for a drink in the old bar where I would unwind. I thought it would be impolite if I didn't try the Waldorf salad while I stayed at the hotel; I loved every mouthful and can see why it has stood the test of time.

Make the dressing by combining all the ingredients in an screw-top jar and shake until combined.

Leaving the skin on, cut the apple cheeks off the core and thinly slice. Place in a bowl with the celery and lemon juice, then mix together. Roughly chop half of the toasted walnuts and add them to the mixture.

Roughly chop the celery leaves and fold into the salad with 2 tablespoons of the vinaigrette.

Loosely arrange the witlof on a platter and spoon the apple–celery mixture over the top. Drizzle with more of the dressing and garnish with the remaining toasted walnuts.

MEXICAN BARBECUED CORN COBS

6 SERVES

6 corn cobs in the husk
vegetable oil
100 g (3½ oz) whole-egg mayonnaise
1 handful of washed and picked coriander
   (cilantro) leaves, chopped
1 teaspoon chopped chipotle chillies in
   adobo sauce (see Note)
200 g (7 oz) manchego cheese, very
   finely grated
2 limes, cut into quarters

How good is barbecued corn on the cob!? Corn is my favourite vegetable, and it features in my home cooking on a weekly basis. I love using it in soups, risottos and salsas but my all-time favourite is corn simply cooked on the barbecue with a variety of condiments depending on what style of meal I am cooking. This recipe makes a great addition to any Mexican meal and it's really simple—all you need is some good-quality store-bought mayonnaise (or home-made if you have the time), some chipotle chilli sauce or finely chopped chillies, a squeeze of lime and freshly grated manchego or other cheese.

Boil the corn cobs in their husks in a large saucepan of boiling water until just tender. Refresh in iced water. Pull the husk away from the cob leaving it still attached at the base.

Preheat a barbecue hotplate or chargrill to high. Lightly brush the corn with a little oil and season with salt and freshly ground black pepper. Cook on the barbecue for 3 minutes on each side.

Combine the mayonnaise, coriander and chilli. Spread the mayonnaise over the hot corn, sprinkle with the grated cheese and serve with lime wedges.

Note: Chipotle chillies in adobo sauce are available at speciality food stores.

ROASTED POTATOES WITH GARLIC AND ROSEMARY

4 SERVES

900 g (2 lb) large new potatoes cut into
2.5 cm (1 inch) dice, skins on
1 bunch of rosemary, leaves picked
2 bulbs of garlic, cloves separated, skins
left on
100 ml (3½ fl oz) olive oil

This probably doesn't need a recipe or belong in a cookbook since we are only using three main ingredients—potatoes, garlic and rosemary—but the book is titled *My Kitchen* and this is something I cook at least once every fortnight with a roast. My kids go nuts for these potatoes and more surprisingly for the roasted garlic. They are now eating a bulb (not a clove but a bulb) of garlic at every roast dinner. I feel sorry for their teachers and classmates the next day, but since garlic is one of the world's superfoods I am stoked they love it.

Preheat the oven to 180°C (350°F/Gas 4). Line a large roasting tin with baking paper.

Put the potatoes in a saucepan of cold water and bring to the boil. Cook on the boil for 5 minutes, then drain.

Place the potatoes, rosemary, garlic and oil into the roasting tin and mix until the oil coats the potatoes. Season with salt and freshly ground black pepper. Cover with foil and place in the oven and cook for 30 minutes.

Remove the foil and toss the potatoes so they will cook evenly. Return to the oven without the foil and allow to cook for a further 15 minutes, or until tender in the middle and crispy on the outside. Once cooked, season with more salt and freshly ground black pepper and arrange on a large dish to serve.

BROCCOLINI WITH LEMON AND GARLIC

4 SERVES

2 bunches of broccolini
3 tablespoons extra virgin olive oil
2 garlic cloves, chopped
zest and juice of 1 lemon

How many people simply boil their vegetables and plop them on the plate? I know I have been guilty of this in the past but I regretted it as soon as I took my first bite. Now I make sure to give my broccoli, carrot, cauliflower, beans or peas a little bit of love before they go from the pot to the plate. There are so many easy ways you can make your vegetables shine. This is my tried and tested technique—good olive oil, garlic, salt and pepper and a squeeze of lemon. Voila!

Cut the stem end off the broccolini. Blanch the broccolini in boiling water for 3-4 minutes or until tender. Drain.

Meanwhile, heat the oil in a frying pan over medium heat, add the garlic and cook until it starts to colour lightly and become fragrant.

Add the broccolini to the frying pan and sauté for 2 minutes, then add the lemon zest, juice, salt and freshly ground black pepper.

POLENTA CHIPS WITH MUM'S OLD-FASHIONED TOMATO SAUCE AND GARLIC AÏOLI

6 SERVES

POLENTA CHIPS
20 g (¾ oz) butter
1.25 litres (5 cups) water
250 g (9 oz/1⅔ cups) instant polenta
100 g (3½ oz/1 cup) freshly grated
   parmesan
vegetable oil, for deep-frying
75 g (2½ oz/½ cup) plain (all-purpose) flour
extra 75 g (2½ oz/½ cup) instant polenta
2 tablespoons finely chopped flat-leaf
   (Italian) parsley

These polenta chips are the ones we serve at Hugos Manly. Like the chips in all our restaurants, they are served with my mum's tomato sauce, though I have tinkered with her recipe slightly (sorry, Mum) by adding tamarind because I like the slightly sour tang it gives to the sauce.

Line a 30 x 20 cm (12 x 8 inch) baking tin with baking paper.

To make the polenta chips, start by cooking the polenta. Put the butter and water in a medium–large saucepan and bring up to a simmer; do not let the water boil, as polenta will go lumpy when added to boiling water. Slowly pour in the polenta and stir well to avoid the polenta getting lumpy—it will begin to thicken immediately. Cook for 5–8 minutes, stirring continuously. When you see the polenta coming away from the sides of the pan, you will know it is done. Remove the pan from the heat, add half of the parmesan and stir well. Season with salt and freshly ground black pepper.

Pour the polenta mixture into the lined baking tin and smooth out evenly using a wet spoon or palette knife—it should be about 2 cm (¾ inch) thick. Allow the polenta to cool completely—this could take up to 1 hour.

Once the polenta mixture is cool, gently remove the set polenta by flipping the tin upside down onto a chopping board. Remove the baking paper and cut the polenta into 5 x 2 cm (2 x ¾ inch) strips.

Preheat the oil in your deep-fryer to 180°C (350°F) or fill a large heavy-based saucepan one-third full of oil and heat until it reaches the correct temperature.

Combine the flour and extra polenta in a bowl, add some of the polenta strips and lightly coat. Cook in batches in the hot oil for 2–3 minutes, or until golden. Drain on paper towel, then place in a large bowl. Toss the chips with the remaining parmesan and sprinkle with parsley. Season with salt and serve with home-made tomato sauce and home-made garlic aïoli (see opposite).

AÏOLI

4 free-range egg yolks

50 g (1¾ oz) garlic confit or roasted
  garlic cloves

2 teaspoons dijon mustard

2 tablespoons lemon juice

200 ml (7 fl oz) vegetable oil

MUM'S OLD-FASHIONED
TOMATO SAUCE

1½ tablespoons olive oil

1½ onions, roughly chopped

3 garlic cloves, minced

¼ bunch of thyme, chopped

¼ bunch of rosemary, chopped

500 g (1 lb 2 oz) tomatoes, roughly chopped

1 green apple, roughly chopped

1½ tablespoons tomato paste (concentrated
  purée)

1 tablespoon tamarind concentrate

200 ml (7 fl oz) tomato sauce (ketchup)

To make the aïoli, place the egg yolks, garlic, mustard, lemon juice and some salt in a jug. Using a hand-held blender start blending, adding the oil gradually until creamy. Season with salt and freshly ground black pepper.

To make the tomato sauce, heat the olive oil in a frying pan over low-medium heat. Add the onion, garlic, thyme and rosemary and gently sweat the onion. Add the tomato and apple and cook out the liquid stirring occasionally.

Add the tomato paste, tamarind and tomato sauce, bring to the boil then reduce to a simmer for 15-20 minutes.

Cool the mixture slightly, then transfer to a blender and blend to a purée and season to taste. Pass through a medium-fine chinois.

Store any leftovers in sterilised jars—this sauce will keep for about 10 days in the refrigerator.

ASIAN COLESLAW

4 SERVES

DRESSING
80 ml (2½ fl oz/⅓ cup) grapeseed oil
1 tablespoon sesame oil
50 ml (1½ fl oz) light soy sauce
1½ tablespoons organic honey
1 tablespoon mirin
juice of 1 lemon

½ savoy cabbage, finely shredded
¾ purple cabbage, finely shredded
sea salt flakes
4 Lebanese (short) cucumbers, halved
    lengthways, seeds removed and
    thinly sliced
2 carrots, coarsely grated
1 bunch of mint, washed and picked
1 bunch of coriander (cilantro), leaves
    washed and picked
1 tablespoon white sesame seeds, toasted
1 tablespoon black sesame seeds

The humble cabbage is an underrated and underused vegetable, which is hard to understand as cabbages are cheap and available all year round. This crunchy, easy, healthy coleslaw is a good alternative to a leafy salad. You can use red or white cabbages or a combination of both and change the herbs to create your own version. This salad will work with just about anything off the barbecue—fish, chicken or steak. For extra crunch, toss in some crisp-fried shallots at the last minute.

To make the dressing, whisk together all the ingredients and season with salt and freshly ground black pepper. Set aside.

Combine the cabbage and season with salt flakes. Add the dressing, then gently toss through the cucumber, carrot, mint and coriander. To finish, sprinkle with white and black sesame seeds.

PARSNIP AND CELERIAC GRATIN

6–8 SERVES

1 knob of butter
4 bulbs of garlic, peeled
400 ml (14 fl oz) cream
8 sprigs of thyme
2 large celeriacs, peeled
8 large parsnips, peeled

BREADCRUMB TOPPING

120 g (4¼ oz/1½ cups) sourdough
    breadcrumbs
1 tablespoon picked thyme
2 tablespoons chopped flat-leaf (Italian)
    parsley
1 long red chilli, seeds removed and
    finely diced
3 tablespoons olive oil

Parsnips start to appear in the cooler months and cooking them in a gratin reminds me of winter, open fires and a nice bottle of red wine. You don't need to be an expert with a knife to create dishes like this—if you master the use of a mandolin (available at all kitchen shops) paper-thin slices of vegetables are easily achievable without loss of fingers. I have combined celeriac and parsnip here, but you can make a gratin with layers of desiree potato and celeriac, or try sweet potato and onion with some fresh sage leaves. Cooked in garlic-infused cream the vegetables melt in your mouth with a lovely crunchy crust. Serve the gratin alongside your favourite roast—you can't beat it.

Preheat the oven to 160°C (315°F/Gas 2–3) and rub a roasting tin (about 20 x 30 cm/8 x 12 inches) with butter.

Smash the garlic cloves and place in a saucepan with the cream and thyme, then season with salt and freshly ground black pepper. Slowly heat the cream and simmer for 5 minutes, without allowing it to boil. Take the pan off the heat to allow the flavours to infuse for 20 minutes while preparing the gratin.

Cut the celeriac in half. Using a mandolin, slice the parsnips and celeriac into paper-thin slices—as the slices come off the mandolin, arrange them neatly in rows in the prepared tin until a complete layer is formed, creating a fanned effect. Continue making layers until all the celeriac and parsnip have been used, seasoning each layer with a touch of salt and freshly ground black pepper.

Pour the cream through a sieve over the vegetables—they should be wet but not entirely submerged. Cover the tin tightly with foil and bake for 1¼ hours.

Meanwhile, to make the breadcrumb topping, combine the breadcrumbs, herbs, chilli and oil and mix well.

Remove the gratin from the oven. Increase the oven temperature to 180°C (350°F/Gas 4), remove the foil from the gratin, spread the breadcrumb mixture over the top and continue to cook for an extra 15 minutes, or until golden brown.

SNAKE BEANS WITH CHILLI PASTE

4 SERVES

CHILLI PASTE
200 g (7 oz) long red chillies, seeds removed
   and chopped
1 tablespoon diced fresh ginger
2 garlic cloves, roughly chopped
15 g (½ oz) dried shrimp, soaked in hot
   water for 1 hour, then drained
30 g (1 oz) dried fish or scallops, soaked in
   hot water for 1 hour, then drained
1 teaspoon salt
1 teaspoon sugar
80 ml (2½ fl oz/⅓ cup) vegetable oil

400 g (14 oz) snake (yard-long) beans
2 tablespoons vegetable oil
1 garlic clove, minced
1 red chilli, thinly sliced
1 spring onion (scallion), finely diced
100 ml (3½ fl oz) chilli paste (see recipe
   above)

I love the Asian method of stir-frying vegetables and tossing them with strong flavours, such as chilli, garlic and ginger. Keep the leftover chilli paste and add it to some clams or your favourite Asian vegetables when you want a spicy kick.

To make the chilli paste, blend all the ingredients in a food processor, then transfer to a wok over a very low heat and cook for 15 minutes to enhance the flavours without burning. Keep any remaining paste, covered with a thin layer of oil in the refrigerator for up to 1 week.

Cook the snake beans in boiling water for 3 minutes or until tender. Drain well.

Meanwhile, heat the oil in a wok and fry the garlic and chilli for 1 minute or until the garlic starts to colour.

Add the beans, spring onion and chilli paste and sauté for a further 2 minutes. Season with salt and freshly ground black pepper.

JAPANESE DAIKON SALAD

4–6 SERVES

DRESSING

50 ml (1½ fl oz) soy sauce
50 ml (1½ fl oz) rice vinegar
2 teaspoons water
½ teaspoon sugar
pinch of salt
¼ teaspoon mustard powder
pinch of freshly ground pepper
1 tablespoon grapeseed oil
1 tablespoon sesame oil

100 g (3½ oz/2 cups) baby English
    spinach leaves
½ carrot, julienned
20 cm (8 inch) length of daikon (giant
    white radish), thinly sliced into ribbons
½ punnet of alfalfa sprouts
⅓ cup julienned beetroot (beet)
2 tomatoes, cut into quarters
2 tablespoons pine nuts, toasted
2 teaspoons sesame seeds, toasted

I have been fascinated by daikon for over 20 years and whenever I go into a sushi bar or restaurant I admire the chefs' precise daikon slicing technique. Daikon can be braised and it is a great addition to a seafood or meat dish; it can also be served raw. This simple salad is one of my favourite ways to serve daikon—put as much or as little daikon in as you see fit and if you can't find any at the market you can easily substitute normal radish. Kanpai! (Cheers in Japanese.)

To make the dressing, combine all the ingredients in a screw-top jar and shake until well mixed.

Dress the spinach leaves with the dressing and arrange on a platter. Add a layer of carrot and daikon and spoon some more dressing over the top.

Scatter with the alfalfa and beetroot, then top with the tomato, pine nuts and sesame seeds.

QUINOA, RED RICE, CARROT AND PISTACHIO SALAD

4 SERVES

100g (3½ oz) Camargue red rice (see Note)
100 g (3½ oz/½ cup) quinoa
2 tablespoons olive oil
1 brown onion, sliced
60 g (2¼ oz) pistachios
1 large carrot, grated
100 g (3½ oz/2 cups) baby English spinach
   leaves, thinly sliced
4 spring onions (scallions), thinly sliced
100 g (3½ oz) dried apricots, roughly
   chopped
1 handful of mint

DRESSING

90 ml (3 fl oz) olive oil
finely grated zest and juice of 1 orange
2 teaspoons lemon juice
1 garlic clove, minced

I'm always looking for ways to make the dinner table a healthier and more interesting place, not only for myself but for my kids. A good way of achieving this is through the use of salads—this is a wonderful salad that includes some of the world's wonder foods: quinoa, red rice and nuts. Red rice is a wholegrain rice renowned for its delicious flavour and excellent health benefits. Its red colouring is the result of natural pigments contained in its pericap. This salad is a tasty accompaniment to meals from nearly every cuisine. Don't stick to my recipe—have some fun with the ingredients and create your own super salad!

Preheat the oven to 180°C (350°F/Gas 4).

Cook the red rice in boiling salted water for 45 minutes, or until cooked. Drain and allow to cool. At the same time, bring a large saucepan of water to the boil, add the quinoa and simmer for 12-14 minutes, or until cooked. Drain and allow to cool.

Meanwhile, heat the oil in a small saucepan over medium heat and cook the onion, stirring occasionally, for 10-15 minutes, or until soft and caramelised. At the same time, place the pistachios on a baking tray and cook in the oven for 8 minutes, or until lightly toasted. Roughly chop.

To make the dressing, combine the ingredients and set aside.

Place the quinoa, rice and onion in a large bowl, add the remaining ingredients, drizzle with the dressing and mix together to completely coat with the dressing.

Note: Camargue red rice is available from speciality food stores. You can use brown rice or wild rice instead of Camargue.

DESSERTS

04

PEAR, APPLE AND CINNAMON PAN SOUFFLE

4–6 SERVES

CINNAMON CARAMEL
110 g (3¾ oz/½ cup) firmly packed soft
   brown sugar
30 g (1 oz) butter, softened
1 tablespoon water
½ teaspoon ground cinnamon

2 granny smith apples
2 large firm beurre bosc pears
50 g (1¾ oz) butter, chopped
3 tablespoons soft brown sugar
4 free-range eggs, separated
1 teaspoon finely grated lemon rind
1 tablespoon organic honey
2 tablespoons rum
½ teaspoon ground cinnamon
250 g (9 oz) mascarpone

You've got to love a good apple dessert, and this one takes the cake. It looks great and will have your family and guests loving your originality. Instead of having to cook individual soufflés, which can be a bit hard to get consistent in some ovens, this is a cheat's way to achieve the beautiful lightness and finesse of a soufflé without the difficulty. You can play around with whatever fruit is in season, but in the winter months it's hard to go past cooked apple and pears spiced with cinnamon.

To make the cinnamon caramel, combine all the ingredients in a small saucepan, then stir until the sugar dissolves and the butter melts. Bring to the boil and simmer, uncovered, until thickened slightly; keep warm.

Peel and core the apples and cut into eighths. Repeat with the pears without peeling them.

Put the butter in a 25 cm (10 inch) non-stick ovenproof frying pan over medium heat. Once the butter has melted, add the fruit and pan-fry until golden and starting to soften. Add half of the sugar and cook until caramelised.

In a large bowl, whisk the egg yolks with the lemon rind, honey, rum and cinnamon. Beat the egg whites and remaining sugar in a clean bowl using an electric mixer until soft peaks form.

Fold the egg white mixture into the egg yolk mixture and pour over the fruit in the frying pan. Shake the pan slightly to allow the mixture to settle around the fruit. Cook over medium heat until the mixture starts to set.

Meanwhile, preheat the grill (broiler) to very hot. Place the pan under the grill and cook until lightly browned on the top. Top with the mascarpone and cinnamon caramel.

8 SERVES

4 free-range egg whites

170 g (5¾ oz/¾ cup) caster (superfine)
    sugar

1 teaspoon vanilla extract

1 teaspoon white vinegar

1 teaspoon cornflour (cornstarch)

30 g (1 oz/½ cup) shredded coconut

200 ml (7 fl oz) thick (double/heavy) cream

1 mango, peeled and thinly sliced

2 tablespoons passionfruit pulp

PASSIONFRUIT PAVLOVA ROLL

Traditionally, pavlovas are a mixture of egg whites and sugar whisked together then baked until soft and marshmallowy in the centre with a thin, hard crust on the outside, served with whipped cream and an assortment of fruit. The thing that has put me off over the years is the type of fruit normally served with the pav. Here I have adapted the pavlova into a roll and used the two fruits that I think have the right amount of sharpness to balance out the sweetness and richness of the meringue and cream: passionfruit and mango.

Preheat the oven to 140°C (275°F/Gas 1). Grease a 38 x 26 cm (15 x 10½ inch) Swiss roll (jelly roll) tin, then line with a piece of baking paper, allowing it to overhang on the two long sides.

Beat the egg whites in a small bowl using an electric mixer until soft peaks form; gradually add the sugar, beating until it is dissolved before adding the next lot. Fold in the vanilla, vinegar and cornflour.

Spread the mixture into the prepared tin; sprinkle with the coconut. Bake on the lower shelf of the oven for about 15 minutes or until the meringue is browned lightly.

Remove the meringue from the oven. Place a sheet of baking paper (a little larger than the tin) on top of the cooked meringue, then top with a damp kitchen cloth. Flip the tin over. Spray one side of another sheet of baking paper with cooking oil spray and place the greased side down on top of the marshmallowy side of the meringue. Starting with the long end nearest to you, carefully roll up the roulade while it is warm. Set aside to cool while still rolled up.

Carefully unroll the cooled meringue, remove the baking paper and gently spread with the cream. Top with mango and passionfruit. Firmly roll up the meringue. Transfer to a platter and serve.

Note: You will need about two large passionfruit for this recipe, which can be made up to 6 hours ahead.

YOGHURT PANNA COTTA WITH BLUEBERRIES

8 SERVES

375 ml (13 fl oz/1½ cups) cream
1 vanilla bean, split and scraped
115 g (4 oz/½ cup) caster (superfine) sugar
2 teaspoons powdered gelatine
2 tablespoons water
560 g (1 lb 4 oz/2¼ cups) plain yoghurt

BLUEBERRY SAUCE

220 g (7¾ oz/1 cup) caster (superfine) sugar
125 ml (4 fl oz/½ cup) water
3 tablespoons sparkling or white wine
1 vanilla bean, split and scraped
1 cinnamon stick
1 star anise
375 g (13 oz) frozen blueberries
1–2 tablespoons lemon juice

The easiest and most beautiful dessert in the world is panna cotta, which basically means cream that has been set. It was the first dessert I learned to make as an apprentice and I used to love making it because I knew it was very hard to get it wrong, which meant that I didn't get in trouble from the head chef. I have served yoghurt panna cottas here with blueberries as I love the flavour of lightly warmed and infused blueberries but feel free to try them with any fruit you like.

Combine half the cream with the vanilla bean, vanilla seeds and sugar in a saucepan. Bring slowly to the boil, stirring constantly, until the sugar dissolves.

Sprinkle the gelatine over the water in a heatproof cup or jug. Place the cup of gelatine mixture in a small saucepan of gently simmering water, without letting the water spill into the cup. Alternatively, microwave it on HIGH (100%) for about 20 seconds, until dissolved.

Stir the gelatine into the cream mixture. (If using leaf gelatine, soften in cold water for 5 minutes, squeeze out the excess water, then add to the cream mixture and stir until dissolved.) Pour the hot cream mixture into a heatproof bowl. Remove the vanilla bean and cool to room temperature. Gradually stir the yoghurt into the cooled cream mixture.

Beat the remaining cream in a small bowl using an electric mixer until soft peaks form. Gently fold the whipped cream into the yoghurt mixture. Spoon the mixture into eight lightly oiled 125 ml (4 fl oz/½ cup) capacity glasses or moulds; cover and refrigerate for 4 hours or overnight.

Meanwhile, to make the blueberry sauce, combine the sugar and water in a small saucepan and stir over low heat, without boiling, until the sugar dissolves. Bring to the boil; boil, uncovered for about 8 minutes or until honey-coloured. Carefully add the wine, vanilla bean and seeds, cinnamon, star anise and blueberries; cook gently for 2 minutes. Remove from the heat. Add the lemon juice to taste; cool to room temperature. Remove the spices.

Serve the panna cottas with the blueberry sauce.

Note: If you want to turn out the panna cotta, make the mixture a little firmer by using 3 teaspoons of gelatine.

GABE'S LEMON–LIME CHEESECAKE

10–12 SERVES

250 g (9 oz) plain biscuits (cookies)
2 tablespoons firmly packed soft brown
    sugar
125 g (4½ oz) unsalted butter
3 x 250 g (9 oz) packets of cream cheese,
    at room temperature
220 g (7¾ oz/1 cup) caster (superfine) sugar
2 limes
1 small lemon
½ teaspoon vanilla extract
3 free-range eggs
1 free-range egg yolk
125 ml (4 fl oz/½ cup) cream
whipped cream, to serve
zest of 1 lemon and 1 lime, for garnish

The thing I love about being a celebrity chef, if that is the correct name for my job, is meeting so many people who have a passion for food, whether it be eating it, cooking it, growing it or producing it. A while ago, I worked with an inspiring couple, Matt Moss and his wife, Gabe, who were kind enough to share the recipe for their cheesecake. I don't normally have a sweet tooth, so as soon as I went back for seconds, I knew it was a hit.

Preheat the oven to 180°C (350°F/Gas 4). Grease the base and side of a 28 cm (11¼ inch) spring-form cake tin with butter. Line the base with baking paper.

Process the biscuits and brown sugar in a food processor until crumbs form. Melt the butter, then add it to the crumb mixture and pulse until combined.

Lightly press the biscuit mixture into the base of the spring-form tin using the base of a glass to compress the mixture and even out the layer of biscuit. Refrigerate for at least 1 hour, or until firm.

Beat the cream cheese and caster sugar using an electric mixer until smooth. Grate the rind of the limes and the lemon over the cream cheese mixture, then squeeze the juice from the limes and lemon. Pour the strained citrus juice and the vanilla into the cream cheese mixture and beat on low until you have a smooth consistency. Add the eggs one at a time until combined. Beat in the egg yolk, then beat in the cream.

Carefully cover the outside base of the tin with foil and place on a baking tray. Pour the cream cheese mixture into the prepared base. Bake the cheesecake for 10 minutes, then reduce the heat to 150°C (300°F/Gas 2) and cook for 30-40 minutes until the mixture has slightly browned.

Remove the cheesecake from the oven and allow to cool, then refrigerate for at least 4 hours until set.

Just before serving, top each slice of cheesecake with a dollop of cream and a little lemon and lime zest.

HONEYCOMB AND ANZAC COOKIE ICE CREAM SANDWICH

4 SERVES

ANZAC COOKIES

75 g (2½ oz/½ cup) plain (all-purpose) flour

95 g (3¼ oz/½ cup lightly packed) soft brown sugar

50 g (1¾ oz/½ cup) rolled (porridge) oats

3 tablespoons shredded coconut

60 g (2¼ oz) unsalted butter

1 tablespoon golden syrup, organic honey or treacle

2 teaspoons water

¼ teaspoon bicarbonate of soda (baking soda)

ICE CREAM

475 ml (16 fl oz) milk

235 ml (7¾ fl oz) thick cream

1 vanilla bean, split and scraped

4 free-range egg yolks

100 g (3½ oz) caster (superfine) sugar

100 g (3½ oz) chocolate-coated honeycomb pieces, chopped

2 Anzac cookies, chopped (see above)

This is a fun twist on an Aussie favourite—Anzac cookies. I love the chewiness of the golden syrup and crunch from the toasted oats mixed in with the vanilla ice cream. Make sure the cookies are cool before you use them or you will have a soggy mess, and make the biscuits a bit thicker that normal for the best results. Kids will love making these.

To make the Anzac cookies, preheat the oven to 175°C (350°F/Gas 3). Lightly grease two baking trays. Sift the flour into a bowl. Add the sugar, rolled oats and coconut.

Melt the butter in a small saucepan over low heat and add the golden syrup, honey or treacle and water. Stir the bicarbonate of soda into the liquid mixture. Add the liquid to the dry ingredients and mix thoroughly. Roll out ten balls the size of golf balls and lay on the trays, allowing room for spreading. Bake for 15 minutes, or until golden. Cool on the trays.

To make the ice cream, put the milk, cream and vanilla in a saucepan over medium heat. Whisk together to distribute the specks of vanilla. Once the mixture is hot enough for foam to form around the edges, remove the pan from the heat.

In a large bowl, whisk the egg yolks and sugar until pale and thick. Gradually pour the hot milk into the egg yolk mixture, whisking constantly. Return the mixture to the saucepan; cook over medium heat, stirring with a wooden spoon until the mixture gels slightly and coats the back of the spoon. Pour the mixture through a sieve or fine strainer into a bowl. Cover, and chill for several hours or overnight.

Pour the mixture into an ice-cream maker and churn according to the manufacturer's instructions. Transfer to a sealed container, and freeze until firm. If the ice cream is too firm, put it in the refrigerator until it softens. Add the honeycomb and Anzac cookie pieces to the ice cream and fold through.

Place scoops of ice cream onto half the cookies and top with the remaining cookies.

OPEN CHERRY PIE

8 SERVES

250 g (9 oz/1⅔ cups) plain (all-purpose)
  flour
2 tablespoons icing (confectioners')
  sugar mixture
pinch of salt
100 g (3½ oz) chilled butter, chopped
100 g (3½ oz) chilled cream cheese,
  chopped
½ teaspoon vanilla bean paste
about 3 tablespoons chilled water
milk, to brush
2 tablespoons sugar

CHERRY FILLING

800 g (1 lb 12 oz) cherries, pitted (about
  600 g/1 lb 5 oz pitted weight)
115 g (4 oz/½ cup) caster (superfine) sugar
3 tablespoons finely grated dark chocolate
½ teaspoon mixed spice
½ teaspoon vanilla bean paste
1 tablespoon lemon juice
2 tablespoons arrowroot or cornflour
  (cornstarch)

A few years ago I was lucky enough to work with a unique culinary talent—Sammie Coryton. She has a wonderfully playful relationship with food preparation that I'm in awe of. This pie is one of my favourite recipes of hers. If you love desserts that are full of flavour and that have everyone wanting more, then this is it. I've served this pie to many friends in my own home and it always gets a very enthusiastic reaction. Sammie is now an owner of a majestic castle in the English countryside called Pentillie Estate where she caters for weddings with her scrumptious food, so if you are getting hitched and want to ensure the food is top-notch, make sure to look her up.

Combine the flour, icing sugar mixture and a pinch of salt in a food processor and process briefly until combined. Add the butter, cream cheese and vanilla. Process until the mixture is just combined and resembles very coarse breadcrumbs. Add about half of the water and process until the mixture just comes together. If you need to add more water, add a few drops at a time. Tip onto a lightly floured workbench and knead briefly until smooth (the dough will be quite soft). Shape into a flat disc and wrap in plastic wrap; refrigerate for 1 hour. Meanwhile, preheat the oven to 220°C (425°F/Gas 7) and lightly grease a large baking tray.

Make the cherry filling just before needed. Put all the ingredients in a large bowl and stir to combine.

Roll the pastry out to a circle about 40-45 cm (16-17¾ inches) in diameter; do not trim. Carefully lift the pastry onto the baking tray. Pile the filling into the centre of the pastry (in a mound about 20 cm/8 inches in diameter) and bring the pastry edges up over the top of the cherries, leaving an opening. Brush the exposed pastry with a little milk, then sprinkle with sugar. Bake for 20 minutes, then reduce the temperature to 190°C (375°F/Gas 5) and bake for a further 30 minutes, or until the pastry is golden. Cover the pie with foil if it's browning too quickly.

Serve the pie with vanilla bean ice cream or cream, if you like.

PETE'S FAMOUS ROCKY ROAD

4–6 SERVES

500 g (1 lb 2 oz) dark chocolate, chopped
400 g (14 oz) large pink and white
   marshmallows
300 g (10½ oz) Turkish delight, chopped
   into small dice
125 g (4½ oz) pistachio nuts, roasted

I've been making rocky road for so long now I can't even remember the first one I ever made. Over time I have perfected the recipe and I am particular about the type of chocolate to use, the size of the marshmallows to make it nice and light, the nut to use (pistachio of course) and the correct amount of Turkish delight so as to not overpower it. These days I only make it at home every once in a while but I do make it professionally and sell it at my partner, Astrid's, chocolate shop and it is one of the most sought after items.

Line a square 15 cm (6 inch) tin with baking paper.

   Melt the chocolate in a heatproof bowl over a saucepan of simmering water on the stovetop, making sure the bowl doesn't touch the water.

   Mix the other ingredients together in a large bowl, then pour the melted chocolate over the top and mix together. Transfer the mixture into the prepared tin and press down gently—it should be about 2.5 cm (1 inch) thick. Allow to set for 3 hours before cutting into logs or pieces.

6 SERVES

500 ml (17 fl oz/2 cups) milk
500 ml (17 fl oz/2 cups) cream
80 g (2¾ oz/⅓ cup) caster (superfine) sugar
1 bay leaf
2 long strips of lemon rind, removed with a
    vegetable peeler
¼ teaspoon ground black pepper
1 teaspoon vanilla extract or 1 vanilla bean,
    split and scraped
120 g (4¼ oz/½ cup) white medium-grain
    rice

POACHED RHUBARB
250 ml (9 fl oz/1 cup) red wine (such
    as shiraz)
230 g (8 oz/1 cup) caster (superfine) sugar
125 ml (4 fl oz/½ cup) water
400 g (14 oz) rhubarb, trimmed, cut into
    6 cm (2½ inch) lengths

RICE PUDDING WITH RED WINE POACHED RHUBARB

I guess I would call this a peasant dish, and peasant dishes are often the yummiest—a recipe using a few basic ingredients cooked with love and passed down from generation to generation. Rice pudding is a dessert that reminds me of childhood—here I have teamed it with rhubarb as I love the flavour and colour after slow cooking it with spices.

Preheat the oven to 160°C (315°F/Gas 2–3). Combine the milk, cream, sugar, bay leaf, lemon rind, pepper and vanilla in a saucepan. Bring to the boil, stirring to dissolve the sugar. Add the rice, stir well and remove from the heat.

Tip the rice mixture into a 2 litre (8 cup) capacity baking dish, then cover with foil. Bake for about 1 hour, stirring occasionally, until the rice is tender and most of the liquid has been absorbed. The rice will absorb any extra liquid on standing, so don't panic unless it's swimming in milk. If this is the case, bake for a further 10 minutes.

Meanwhile, to make the poached rhubarb, bring the wine, sugar and water to the boil; simmer, uncovered, for 10 minutes. Add the rhubarb and return to the boil. Remove immediately from the heat and stand until cold. Carefully remove the cooked rhubarb from the poaching juices using a slotted spoon. Bring the poaching liquid back to the boil and simmer, uncovered, until reduced by two-thirds.

Serve the rice pudding with the poached rhubarb and drizzle with some of the poaching liquid.

21 EBELSKIVERS

400 g (14 oz) bittersweet chocolate,
 roughly chopped or broken
150 g (5½ oz/1 cup) plain (all-purpose)
 flour
1½ teaspoons sugar
1 teaspoon cayenne pepper
½ teaspoon baking powder
¼ teaspoon salt
2 free-range eggs, separated
250 ml (9 fl oz/1 cup) milk
40 g (1½ oz) butter, melted
½ teaspoon vanilla extract
extra melted butter, for brushing
icing (confectioners') sugar, for dusting

CHILLI–CHOCOLATE EBELSKIVERS

Ebelskivers are traditional Danish pancakes. They are made in a special pan called a monk's pan, which is like a non-stick frying pan with a series of circular indents for the batter. Because of the shape it allows you to add a filling, in this case melted chocolate. If you can't find a ebelskiver pan this recipe will work using small ceramic ramekins cooked in the oven.

Melt the chocolate pieces in a heatproof bowl over a saucepan of simmering water on the stovetop, making sure the bowl doesn't touch the water.

In a large bowl, mix together the flour, sugar, cayenne pepper, baking powder and salt.

In a small bowl, mix the egg yolks, then stir in the milk, melted butter and vanilla. Add the egg mixture to the dry ingredients and use a wooden spoon to stir until well blended—the batter should still be lumpy.

In a clean bowl, whisk the egg whites until stiff. Using a spatula first fold about one-third of the egg white mixture into the batter, then half the melted chocolate. Now add the remaining egg white and mix until no white streaks remain.

Brush the wells of the ebelskiver pan with some melted butter, place over medium heat and, when the butter starts to bubble, spoon 1 tablespoon of the batter into each well. Working quickly, carefully spoon 1 teaspoon of the melted chocolate into the centre of each ebelskiver, then top with another tablespoon of batter.

Cook the bottoms for 3–5 minutes until they are lightly browned, then carefully turn (a skewer can be useful for this) and cook on the other side for another 3 minutes. Dust with icing sugar, then serve while still hot.

Note: If you don't have an ebelskiver pan, you can use 60 ml (2 fl oz/¼ cup) capacity ramekins or small tins in the oven. Put 1 tablespoon of batter in the base of each ramekin, add 1 teaspoon of melted chocolate, then top with another tablespoon of batter. Cook for 5–7 minutes in a 180°C (350°F/Gas 4) oven.

MANGO AND ROSEWATER MASCARPONE PASTRIES

4 SERVES

1 sheet of butter puff pastry, partially thawed

3 tablespoons icing (confectioners') sugar, sifted

200 g (7 oz) mascarpone

2 teaspoons rosewater, or to taste

1 firm ripe mango, thinly sliced

2 tablespoons coarsely chopped toasted pistachio kernels

extra 1 tablespoon icing (confectioners') sugar, for dusting (optional)

I grew up in sunny Queensland so I now have a love affair with anything tropical, from fishing on the reefs to eating mud crabs and tropical fruit. And there is no tropical fruit mightier than the juicy mango—it is great with seafood, wonderful in a smoothie or eaten plain, but I think the best way to eat a ripe mango is in a dessert. This is a lovely little dessert you can easily make at home when mangoes are at their peak.

Preheat the oven to 200°C (400°F/Gas 6). Line one large baking tray with baking paper and have a second tray the same size ready.

Lightly dust the pastry sheet with 2 teaspoons of the icing sugar. Prick the pastry all over with a fork and dust again lightly with another 2 teaspoons of the icing sugar.

Cut the pastry sheet in half. Cut each half into four rectangles. Place the pastry rectangles on the prepared baking tray. Spray a piece of baking paper, the same size as the tray, with some cooking oil spray. Place the paper over the pastry, oiled-side down. Place the second baking tray on top (this will prevent the pastry from rising). Bake for 15–20 minutes, or until the pastry is golden and cooked through. Transfer the pastry rectangles to a wire rack to cool.

Combine the mascarpone, remaining 2 tablespoons of icing sugar and the rosewater in a bowl, and stir gently until just combined.

To serve, spread the mascarpone mixture over four of the pastry rectangles and top with the mango and pistachios. Dust the other squares with icing sugar and wave a cook's blowtorch over them to form a shiny glaze. Put these on top of the mango and pistachios.

CRANBERRY AND COINTREAU GRANITA

4 SERVES

SUGAR SYRUP
100 g (3½ oz) caster (superfine) sugar
100 ml (3½ fl oz) water

500 ml (17 fl oz/2 cups) cranberry juice
125 ml (4 fl oz/½ cup) Cointreau
25 ml (1 fl oz) strained lime juice
25 ml (1 fl oz) strained fresh orange juice
3 tablespoons sugar syrup (see above)

CRANBERRY COMPOTE
250 g (9 oz/1⅔ cups) sweetened dried
   cranberries
100 g (3½ oz) caster (superfine) sugar
200 ml (7 fl oz) cranberry juice

Most of the things that bring a smile to my face are simple: surfing, spending time with my kids, fishing, building a campfire in the mountains, snorkelling over a coral reef alive with sea life, listening to someone playing an acoustic guitar and, of course, preparing simple meals. The simplest desserts I make are granitas—basically frozen little rocks. I use fruit juice and add sugar syrup and a splash of alcohol that complements the flavour of the juice. Once this is frozen you have the perfect dessert to serve on a hot summer's day or on any day after a big dinner—it refreshes the palate and leaves you feeling cleansed.

To make the sugar syrup, place the sugar and water in a small saucepan over low heat and stir until the sugar dissolves. Increase the heat and bring to the boil. Remove the pan from the heat and set aside to cool.

Mix the cranberry juice, Cointreau, lime juice, orange juice and the 3 tablespoons of sugar syrup together and taste before freezing, adjusting if necessary.

Pour the mixture into a shallow tray and freeze for a few hours. Run a fork through it so it resembles ice shavings.

Meanwhile, to make the cranberry compote, place the cranberries, sugar and cranberry juice in a saucepan and cook until the liquid has reduced and thickened slightly. Allow to cool completely.

Serve the compote with the granita.

1 tablespoon soft brown sugar

6 large plums, halved, stones removed

225 g (8 oz) butter, softened

170 g (5¾ oz/¾ cup) caster (superfine) sugar

extra 115 g (4 oz/½ cup firmly packed) soft brown sugar

1 teaspoon vanilla extract

3 free-range eggs

150 g (5½ oz/1 cup) plain (all-purpose) flour

110 g (3¾ oz/¾ cup) self-raising flour

¾ teaspoon bicarbonate of soda (baking soda)

1 teaspoon ground cinnamon

45 g (1½ oz/½ cup) flaked almonds

2 tablespoons milk

whipped cream, to serve

UPSIDE-DOWN PLUM CAKE

This cake is best served warm with whipped cream, although it's also delicious as a tea cake when cold.

Preheat the oven to 140°C (275°F/Gas 1). Grease a deep 22 cm (8½ inch) round cake tin and line the base with baking paper.

Sprinkle the 1 tablespoon of brown sugar over the base of the tin, then arrange the plums, cut side down, on top of the sugar.

Using an electric mixer beat the butter, caster sugar, extra brown sugar and vanilla extract in a bowl until light and fluffy. Add the eggs, then sift in the combined flours, bicarbonate of soda and cinnamon. Beat gently until combined. Add the almonds and milk, then mix until just combined. Spoon the mixture into the prepared tin and spread evenly over the plums.

Bake for 1 hour 20 minutes, or until cooked when tested with a skewer. Stand the cake in the tin for 15 minutes before turning onto a serving plate. Serve warm, accompanied by whipped cream, or cool to room temperature and serve cold.

INDEX

THANKS

I have loved writing this book...it is my favourite so far, but it wouldn't have come together without the many talents of my wonderful team with whom I have the pleasure of working on a daily basis. Kim Lockyer, you are the strongest fighter I know and I am glad you are in my corner on this amazing journey. Monica and Jacinta Cannataci (the wonder twins), you girls never cease to amaze me with your unfaltering work ethic and your infectious smiles. Massimo Mele, Phil Matthews, Kaz Derbas and Matt Drummond, you keep the cogs well greased and moving forward in the Hugos kitchens. My business partners, Dave, Dan, Corsi and Daddy'o, thanks for your ongoing support. My family, Mum, Astrid, Udo, Poldi, Walter and Leonie, you guys rock! And, of course, my little girls, Chilli and Indii, you make me very proud and I love you so much!

The book couldn't have happened without the good crew at Murdoch Books. Juliet, Kay and Kylie, thank you once again for letting me put my thoughts down on paper and thanks to Livia for organising everything for me. Sonia, MJ, Shannon and the rest of the Murdoch crew, you are all such a joy to work with. The true stars of this book are the dynamic duo of Katie Quinn Davies and David Morgan. Katie, your photography makes my food jump off the page and Dave, I love how you can make the simplest dishes look absolutely mouth watering. And to the amazing talents of Reuben Crossman, thanks for making each book look so good. It's my shout next time we are at Hugos.

Published in 2011 by Murdoch Books Pty Limited

Murdoch Books Australia
Pier 8/9
23 Hickson Road
Millers Point NSW 2000
Phone: +61 (0) 2 8220 2000
Fax: +61 (0) 2 8220 2558
www.murdochbooks.com.au

Murdoch Books UK Limited
Erico House, 6th Floor
93–99 Upper Richmond Road
Putney, London SW15 2TG
Phone: +44 (0) 20 8785 5995
Fax: +44 (0) 20 8785 5985
www.murdochbooks.co.uk

Publisher: Kylie Walker
Designer: Reuben Crossman
Photographer: Katie Quinn Davies
Stylist: David Morgan
Project Manager: Livia Caiazzo
Food Editor: Sonia Greig
Editor: Zoë Harpham
Production: Joan Beal

National Library of Australia Cataloguing-in-Publication Data

Author: Evans, Pete.
Title: My kitchen/Pete Evans.
ISBN: 978-1-74196-828-6 (hbk.)
Notes: Includes index.
Subjects: Cooking.

Dewey Number: 641.5
A catalogue record for this book is available from the British Library.

PRINTED BY C&C Offset Printing Co. Ltd., China.

IMPORTANT: Those who might be at risk from the effects of salmonella poisoning (the elderly, pregnant women, young children and those suffering from immune deficiency diseases) should consult their doctor with any concerns about eating raw eggs.

OVEN GUIDE: You may find cooking times vary depending on the oven you are using. For fan-forced ovens, as a general rule, set the oven temperature to 20°C (35°F) lower than indicated in the recipe.